Philip Gw[...] [...]
lived and w[...] [...] [...]
in the 1990s. He first came to Italy in 1994, when he spent some time working for the European Space Agency in Frascati. Philip now lives permanently in Venice, where he works as a teacher, writer and translator. He is the author of the Nathan Sutherland series, which is set in contemporary Venice and which has been translated into several languages, including Italian and German.

PRAISE FOR PHILIP GWYNNE JONES

'A playful novel, recounted by a witty and engaging narrator . . . as Venetian as a painting by Bellini (or a glass of Bellini). Oh, and it's also an unputdownable thriller' – Gregory Dowling, author of *Ascension*, on *The Venetian Game*

'A crime book for people with sophisticated tastes: Venice, opera, renaissance art, good food and wine . . . I enjoyed all that and more' – *The Crime Warp*

'The Venetian setting is vividly described and Gwynne Jones's good, fluent writing makes for easy reading' – Jessica Mann, *Literary Review*

'It is no surprise to find that Philip Gwynne Jones lives in Venice . . . art and architecture interweave into a story that builds to an almost surreal climax' – *Daily Mail*, on *The Venetian Game*

'A civilized, knowledgeable, charming antidote to the darker reaches of the genre, full of entertaining descriptions of the city . . . Lovely. Makes you want to book a flight to Venice straight away' – N J Cooper, Bookoxygen.com

Also by Philip Gwynne Jones

The Venetian Game
Vengeance in Venice
The Venetian Masquerade

Philip Gwynne Jones

To Venice with Love

A Midlife Adventure

CONSTABLE

CONSTABLE

First published in Great Britain in 2019 by Robinson
This paperback edition published in 2020 by Constable

A CIP catalogue record for this book
is available from the British Library.

ISBN: 978-1-47213-022-8

Typeset in Sabon by Hewer Text UK Ltd, Edinburgh
Printed and bound in Great Britain by Clays Ltd, Elcograf S.p.A.

Papers used by Constable are from well-managed
forests and other responsible sources.

Constable
An imprint of
Little, Brown Book Group
Carmelite House
50 Victoria Embankment
London EC4Y 0DZ

An Hachette UK Company
www.hachette.co.uk

www.littlebrown.co.uk

For Caroline. None of this
would be happening without you.

Contents

N

Sant'Ariano

Torcello

Mazzorbetto

Mazzorbo • Burano

Laguna
Veneta

San Giàcomo
in Paludo

Lazzaretto
Nuovo

Murano

• Sant'Erasmo

Le Vignole

Venice

Giudecca

San Lazzaro
degli Armeni

Lido •

Lido di Venezia

Malamocco •

Adriatic
Sea

• Alberoni

0   1   2   3   4   5 km

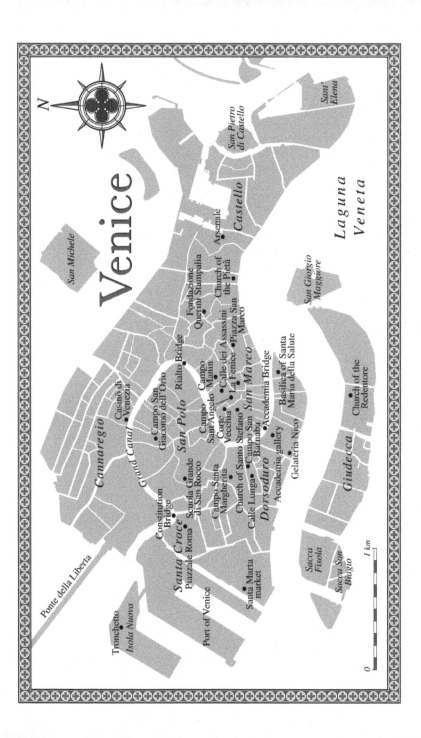

Introduction

At the end of 2011, my wife Caroline and I gave up our jobs in order to move to Venice.

We had no idea if it would be possible to live there full-time, if we would be able to earn a living, whether homesickness would drive us back to the UK or, indeed, how to go about a project such as this.

I set to work trying to find some information that could help us, either in print or on the internet. I found numerous accounts of moving to Italy, but surprisingly few on Venice itself; and even fewer from the perspective of 'normal' people – those who would have to get a regular, non-glamorous job in order to make ends meet.

I decided that, whether it were to be successful or not, the experience would be worth recording, either as a 'how to do it' guide or as a terrible warning to others. In the event, the scope of the book grew as I wrote it, and became the saga of what I once called 'The Venice Project'.

It is not a history of *La Serenissima* – the story of the Most Serene Republic has been written many times, and by writers far more adept than I. Neither is it an art, music or architecture primer. It's the story of what happened to us during the most extraordinary few years of our lives; when we went from nine-to-five jobs to living in the most beautiful city on earth.

This is the story of how we did it; and how we are still, just about, getting away with it.

Prologue

Music has been my great love, ever since I was a kid spending my pocket money on 1970s punk albums that my parents looked on with horror. The New Wave supported me through school, while university was a voyage of discovery into progressive rock. I went through a brief folky phase, complete with Aran jumper. When I started playing guitar in my twenties, I became obsessed with old blues and jazz records.

In the early 1990s, I found myself working on an IT contract for an oil company in Gelsenkirchen, Germany. I was the only Brit in the office, and living in a hotel. Weekends could be lonely and I knew I had to do something other than spend them in the pub with a book.

I discovered that you could go to the opera in Essen for not much more than ten Deutschmarks. I figured I had nothing to lose. My first opera was Wagner's *Tristan und Isolde*. I'd like to say it was a life-changing experience, but the truth is I nodded off during the second act. I knew, however, that this was something I wanted to explore and went back a month later, for *Parsifal*. I stayed awake this time. I had acquired a new obsession.

I spent many years working away from the UK, and frequently on my own. Music – mainly classical by this time – was my travelling companion. Then I moved to Edinburgh in 1996 and ended up staying.

I came to know a group of people – anonymously – via an online classical music chatroom. A number of them were based in Scotland, and we arranged to get together for a few beers in Glasgow. We talked about concerts, recordings and whether it was right for a pub in that particular part of the city to be offering such a thing as a 'Pint and Panini [*sic*]'. It turned out that the meet-up was also a farewell party for one of our number.

He was leaving to move to Spain with his wife. He told me they were going to teach English. Something called TEFL, which I found out stood for Teaching English as a Foreign Language.

I'd never heard of this and thought little more of it until the following year when I ran into him again, this time in a pub in Edinburgh. He was back to visit family for a couple of days. He talked about life in Spain. He seemed happy. I complained about my job. A lot. He put up with this with remarkable patience, went to the bar, returned with a pair of pints and smiled.

'Look, Phil, you've got no kids. You've got no real ties here. You could do this as well, you know. What's keeping you?'

I never saw him again.

Chapter 1

I met Caroline on 23 July 1998. I was living in Edinburgh, had recently finished a contract with Scottish Gas, and was desperately looking for something I could do beyond computer programming. As well as classical music I had become addicted to playing the electric guitar, and I was going to take time off to study it properly.

I'd signed up with the Guitar Institute in London. I'd given notice on my flat, and told my boss I wouldn't be renewing my contract. I'd found a place to live in London, and hired a van.

I was in my mid-thirties, I had only played in covers bands and – in my heart of hearts – I knew I was never going to be more than a competent pub rocker. It was, in retrospect, an insane plan.

On what I thought would be my last ever day of work in the IT industry, I went for a meal with friends, and then on to the pub. People drifted away, until two of us remained. Graeme was a pal from a previous IT job, and we frequently met up over a beer to talk about football and old guitar bands. It was getting late, and the atmosphere was downbeat. We didn't know when we'd next see each other.

'Hi, Graeme.' The speaker was a woman standing at the bar.

'Hi, Caroline.' Graeme dragged a stool over to our table. 'D'you want to join us?'

She came and sat down. She'd been for a drink with her ex, and had decided to stay for one more beer after he'd gone home. Graeme had known her for years and, with impeccable timing, had waited until I'd decided to leave Edinburgh in search of rock stardom before introducing us.

We talked. And then we talked some more. About music and theatre and opera and art, about politics and pubs, and which Bob Dylan album was the best. We discovered we had the same recording of Wagner's Ring Cycle. And at some point we realised that Graeme was no longer there . . .

The next day I rang my landlord and told him I'd changed my mind. I rang my boss and asked if I could have my job back. I lost my deposit on the van and the new flat.

I didn't care. Because I knew that Caroline and I were going to get married . . .

We became engaged that Christmas, and married in 2000. Both of us, for many years, had been freelance IT workers, regularly moving from company to company every couple of years. Caroline – who had studied Prehistory and Archaeology – had ended up in IT by mistake, and was a systems analyst; I was a programmer and discovering that work opportunities were becoming thin on the ground.

Neither of us wanted to work away from home any more, and we decided it was time to settle down in Edinburgh. We were middle-aged, we had no savings, we owned no property.

We needed to start thinking about the future. We would buy a flat and get steady, secure jobs that would see us through to retirement and a comfy pension. We were going to do the right thing. The sensible thing.

We ended up working for the Bank of Scotland.

The roof collapsed in 2008. Despite all assurances to the contrary, everyone at work knew that something was wrong. Each week, an email would arrive from the chief executive, assuring us that we were all doing very well and the bank was going from strength to strength. It didn't fool anyone. The big giveaway was when the mirthless grin on his attached photograph changed to a stern, unsmiling one.

Then, one September afternoon, the BBC website reported that Lloyds Banking Group was seeking permission from the government to relax competition law and proceed with a takeover. The site was quickly blocked and half-hearted denials were posted on the office intranet, but everybody knew that the game was up: in the space of ten years, a bank that predated the 1707 Act of Union between England and Scotland had been run into the ground.

In late 2010 we were told that Caroline's job as a senior analyst was at immediate risk and that mine – a more humble but knuckle-whiteningly stressful position in technical support of financial systems – would also be within twelve months. We faced redundancy, in middle age, in a sector that was dying on its knees. Our flat, bought shortly after joining BoS, was worth less than we had paid for it and our pensions were practically worthless. We had to face the fact that we had been rubbish at capitalism.

Except that, the more we thought about it, the more we wondered why we would want to stay with the bank at all. It hadn't been much of a job for years and, following the takeover, the situation had become progressively worse. We saw a steady stream of friends and colleagues losing their jobs and any job satisfaction was long gone, replaced by the fear of redundancy. We worked in an industry that the public despised. It had become a horrible place to work.

I knew that my best years in IT were over a decade behind me. I was burned out. In my darker moments I felt as if I would be trapped in a job I hated until the stress of it killed me.

Why would we want to stay there? What if we were to try something else?

I remembered the Man in the Pub, and started to think.

I first came to Italy in 1994, when I spent some time working for the European Space Agency in Frascati, a small-ish town in the hills outside of Rome. It sounded like the most exciting job I was ever likely to have. The reality was somewhat different.

I was not designing satellites or Mars probes (to be honest, that was probably for the best). The job could be described as 'collating a list of periodicals and subscribers across various legacy platforms and migrating them into an integrated bespoke system on a distributed client-server architecture'. Or, in plain English, 'taking a lot of old address books and putting them all together'.

It was not the best job in the world, and the project dragged on for six months. I hadn't anticipated that and so, instead of finding an apartment in Rome and enjoying all the capital had to offer, I rented a house in a remote village in the Colli Albani which, I reasoned, would be 'romantic'. I had not thought about the logistics of living in a village with no public transport at the weekends.

Despite an unrewarding job and long late-night walks up narrow and unlit roads, I enjoyed Italy immensely. No, more than that, I *adored* it. I loved walking around the ancient sites of Rome, or taking the train to Florence and realising that every building you entered held something amazing. I enjoyed the company of Italian football fans during the team's doomed but heroic World Cup exploits. If I hadn't quite made the most of the experience, Italy, I knew, was somewhere I wanted to return.

I never did manage it, until I met Caroline. We became engaged while on holiday in the Dolomites, honeymooned in Sicily and kept returning to Italy, year after year. Amalfi and Positano. Naples and Palermo. Rome and Florence and Bologna. Venice. And, always, the same conversation, typically on the last night of the holiday: *Do you think we'll ever be able to move here?*

It seemed impossible. We didn't have the money or the language skills, and I was dubious about the European Space Agency ever taking me back. It would have to be post-retirement, but I wasn't sure we'd ever be able to do that anyway. It was a pipe dream, something to take the edge off going back to work.

But now a Man in a Pub had told me about something called TEFL, and living in Spain while teaching English. What if we were to try this in Italy? With this TEFL thing and a bit of redundancy money, might it be possible?

I spent hours upon hours running the figures through spreadsheets. We could clear our debts, use the remainder to move and attempt to live off whatever income teaching would bring in. The most basic of research indicated that this was not going to be a lot but, if the two of us were bringing in a salary, it started to look feasible. We would have between one and two years of contingency to try to make it work.

There is no easy way to tell your wife that you've had a life-changing idea based on a conversation with a man you met in a pub years ago. I was prepared to laugh it off as a silly joke on my part. And yet, when I explained the figures, Caroline looked at me and said, 'So . . . we could actually *do* this?'

We had a good life in Edinburgh. We had pubs, the theatre, concerts, galleries, plenty of friends. I liked the way we would run into people we knew simply by wandering about the town. I had lived there for nearly twenty years, longer than I had spent anywhere in my life, and the city fitted me like a comfy old pair of shoes. I had never imagined wanting to live elsewhere.

It was a lot to give up. Were we really going to take such a life-changing decision on the basis of something so uncertain? Yet it was a spine-tinglingly exciting idea.

There was no great moment of decision for us, but in the early part of 2011 we tacitly crossed the line from 'Wouldn't it be great if we did this?' to 'We're actually going to do this!'

The Venice Project was born. The next time the bank held a round of voluntary redundancies, we would stick our hands up. We would pool whatever money they gave us and move to Italy to teach English.

It was not risk-free, but we had tried risk-free before and the path of least resistance had led us to the financial services industry. If it worked, the prize was a great one. If it didn't, and we ended up back in the UK – well, we would at least have tried. There would never be a better opportunity of doing something like this.

There was also, of course, the possibility of ending up broke and unemployable. We preferred not to think about that.

Why Venice?

We didn't come for Vivaldi, Gabrieli or Monteverdi. We didn't come for Titian, Tintoretto or Tiepolo. We didn't even come to have a gondola ride. We came for Gilbert and George.

Our first visit to Venice, in 2005, was for the Art Biennale, the huge international contemporary art exhibition that takes over the city every couple of years. We had a week and figured that would be enough. As it turned out, that was scarcely enough time to scratch the surface of the Biennale, let alone the city itself.

The strange thing is, Venice itself didn't make much of an impact on us. I came away with an impression of it being 'quite nice' but little more beyond memories of the suffocating heat of the Arsenale and aching feet. We decided we should come back in a non-Biennale year and see what it was properly like. Or, as I put it, I wanted to look at art by dead people.

Forward to 2006. Our flight from Naples had been delayed for hours. It was past midnight when we arrived at Marco Polo airport in Venice. There were no boats at that time and we didn't have the budget for a water taxi. We took the bus to Piazzale Roma and caught the night vaporetto to the Zattere, and our hotel.

It was 2 a.m. by the time we arrived and, fortunately, the night porter let us in. We barely had the energy to open a bottle of prosecco from the minibar before crashing out.

The next morning, I opened the curtains and gazed at the view across the Giudecca canal to Palladio's Church of Il Redentore, the Redeemer. The sun was shining on the water and I knew I had never seen a more beautiful city in my life. I was beginning to understand why Venice is special. We returned year on year, for longer and longer. If our Italian never improved very much, we started to feel at home in the city and to know our way around; and we could kid ourselves that having a Venezia Unica card – and hence the ability to buy cheaper tickets for the vaporetto – was almost as good as being a resident.

At the end of our last holiday, in July 2011, we took the Alilaguna boat from the Zattere to Marco Polo airport. Caroline, somehow, snoozed the whole way. I leant my face against the window, watching as the city slipped from sight. The unbearable thought had occurred to me that we might never be able to return. If only one of us was able to give up their job, the redundancy wouldn't be enough money to fund The Project, neither would we have the cash to come back on holiday.

We had thought we would go anywhere in Italy where we could find work, but no. It had to be Venice. It had to be The Venice Project.

*   *   *

I'd been spreadsheet-pounding for weeks, trying to work out worst-possible-case scenarios along the lines of 'If we can't find work, how long before we have to give up?'

I looked at our possible redundancy pot and added in what we'd managed to save on overpaying the mortgage. I deducted the cost of clearing all our debts. Then I made a stab at estimating the living cost in Venice. I assumed that neither of us would be able to find work for a year.

It didn't leave a lot left over.

We could soften the blow by renting the flat, but that still wouldn't be enough to cover the mortgage. Did we really want to be over a thousand miles away in the event of problems with the flat or with the tenants? Would the fact that the rendering on the building needed to be replaced – a job that would involve months of scaffolding blocking out the view, ruining the flat's main selling point – make it impossible to let anyway? There was also the not-inconsiderable cost of putting all our furniture into storage.

It was a problem. Not enough to stop us going ahead, but I couldn't shake the feeling that we didn't have sufficient contingency.

We spoke to our next-door neighbour, a young man involved in the property business, with a view to getting his opinion on the best thing to do; and in the hope he'd manage the letting on our behalf. Except that as soon as we told him what we were doing he said he and his partner would like to buy the flat off us.

It was a shock. This had never been part of the plan, not least because nothing was selling in Edinburgh. This was knocking away every support and fall-back position. We'd bought late, at the top of the housing market, and if we cut our losses now the chances of being able to buy anywhere in the future were remote.

Yet when I punched the new figures into the spreadsheet, it became obvious. We'd gain another pot of cash and massively reduce our outgoings. It would give us a degree of comfort. If we couldn't find work in Venice, we would at least have the chance to start again elsewhere.

There was really no decision to be made. We haggled over the price but, realistically, it was the only thing to do. In the middle of a desperate crisis in the housing market, we had been lucky.

That left the question of what to do with our possessions. We'd moved from a spacious rented property into a flat half the size and a third more expensive, for the dubious privilege of being able to say that it was 'ours'. We'd already down-sized significantly and got rid of a lot of our stuff. I'd taken so many boxes of old VHS tapes to the Oxfam shop in Morningside that they'd been able to hold a special SF and horror video sale.

But we still had too much clutter and the cost of storing it was going to be enormous. On a weekend visit, my cousin mentioned that they had some outbuildings that we could use. This was marvellous, but it wouldn't seem fair to take advantage of this for free, surely? Her younger daughter was about to start university and would need a car. We weren't going to need ours in Venice; so they'd take the car off our hands and, in exchange, we could store all our possessions with them. We'd have to transport everything to their house in the New Forest, but it was still a good deal.

We'd been lucky again. It was starting to seem like destiny. Caroline worked an absurd ten-month period of notice as IT staff migrated systems that would ultimately make their own jobs redundant, but became free to work on The Venice Project full time from October 2011.

All I had to do was successfully lose my job. I'd been assigned to a series of dead-end projects throughout the year, all of which had been cancelled within months of initiation. I thought this had to be a good sign. Surely, if they couldn't find me any work during the most intense period of IT activity in a decade, they'd be more than happy to let me go. It seemed unlikely that I'd suddenly become indispensable. In all likelihood they would realise that I'd been bluffing my way through the job for years and this was a gilt-edged opportunity to get rid of me. Nevertheless, the thought that it wouldn't go to plan was costing me more than a few sleepless nights. We needed to get lucky one more time.

A Friday afternoon, late September, 2011 . . .
My manager sat across the table from me and laid out a sheaf of papers. We'd worked together for years, and had always got on well. She'd been sympathetic to the fact that my job had been slowly run down over the previous years, but there was nothing she could do about it. I'd been hoping all day that she'd be able to give me a nod or a wink to tell me everything was going to be OK, but she'd been dragged into meeting after meeting, finally finding a space for me right at the end of the day.

'This bit has to be formal, Phil, as you know.'
I half-nodded. I didn't trust myself to speak.

'I'm pleased to say your application for voluntary redundancy has been accepted.'

I let out a deep sigh. I might have cracked a watery smile, but my main recollection is of trying not to shake. She pushed a sheet of paper towards me.

'This is what we can offer you.'

I read it through. It was almost exactly as I expected. The figure on the bottom line was not huge by any means. Yet again, I ran through the sums in my head.

'You don't have to sign it now. Talk to Caroline first if you like. But if you do sign, you have to be aware that this is final. You won't be able to change your mind.'

For a few seconds I paused. I was certain, so absolutely certain that I wanted this. I had been almost sick with worry that morning, drinking endless coffees and cursing that – having given up years ago – the consolation of a cigarette break was denied me. But, for a moment, I stopped and wondered. If I signed, everything would change. All we'd managed to save over the past few years would be put at risk. There was no certainty that this would work. If it failed, we would not be struggling IT professionals. We would be bankrupt ex-IT professionals, with worthless pensions, facing a bleak future.

The feeling lasted for a few seconds at most. Then the doubt passed and I reached for a pen. My breathing returned to normal, my heartbeat slowed.

'Are you quite sure, Phil?'

My hand was steady and I scrawled my signature. I passed the forms back and slumped in my chair, exhaling heavily.

'Thank you. Really, thank you.'

She smiled. 'I'm glad you're pleased. We'll miss you. Are you off to tell Caroline then?'

'In a minute. I need a coffee first. Actually, I need a drink, but a coffee will do for now.'

I got to my feet, unsteadily, and we shook hands.

'Oh, just one more thing.'

'Yes?'

'I don't suppose I could have gardening leave?'

She laughed and shook her head. 'No.'

'Oh well. It was worth a go.'

I grabbed a coffee and went back to my desk. At this time on Friday, most of my colleagues had left for the weekend. Only a few people were around, and nobody gave me so much as a quizzical glance. I reached for the phone to call Caroline . . .

It was settled. We really were going.

The reaction to our news was mixed. Most people thought it was fantastic. The support we received was touching, and humbling.

There were, of course, a few Jeremiahs. It would have been strange if there hadn't been. There were voices of concern along the lines of 'you'll find it difficult to get work' (a fair point, there was no guarantee of this at all), which we accepted were well-meant; but also some rather strange ones.

'Is Caroline OK with this?' (No, I've made her give up her job and sold the flat against her wishes.)

'Are you Catholic?' (And, on being told no, 'Hmm. It would be better if you were.')

'But Italy is broken!' (Damn, now we've got no jobs and no home, why didn't you tell us earlier?)

There was more than a little validity to the last point. I'd been reading the online Italian papers for a couple of years – it had been a way to pass the time while I waited for my latest project to be cancelled – and by the end of 2011 I was under no illusions about the state of Italy. I became familiar with the phrases *lo Spread vola* and *Borsa crolla*. President Giorgio Napolitano had finally, somehow, persuaded Prime Minister Silvio Berlusconi to resign to spend more time with his lawyers, and installed a technocratic government under the leadership of economist Mario Monti. There was a feeling that at least the grown-ups were in charge again, but there was no getting away from the fact that Italy had (and, indeed, still has) serious economic problems.

But what were we to do? We would have felt better if we were leaving for a country with a booming economy, low unemployment and a prosperous population desperate to spend their spare money on English lessons. But, in the middle of the worst economic crisis of my lifetime, this didn't seem likely in the near future.

It had to be now. We'd often hoped to be able to move to Italy in the future, but could we realistically plan for it? Could we assume we'd have our health? Given the state of our pensions, there was no guarantee of being able to retire at all. If we were moving to a country facing great uncertainties, we were also leaving a deeply unhappy one.

The chances of this opportunity coming along again seemed vanishingly small. It had to be now. *Carpe diem* or, if you prefer, *se non ora, quando*: if not now, when?

Chapter 2

I have always been the dreamer, and Caroline the practical one. If there's a problem to overcome, I'm the one who thinks we'll be able to improvise a way out of it, or that it'll sort itself in its own good time. Caroline plans, designs, schedules and leaves nothing to chance. If I had the vision, or the view from a hill, the plan needed her forensic eye to ensure it had any chance of success. We'd read too many accounts of expat adventures, of people following 'The Dream', that had ended in unhappiness or financial disaster. If we were to succeed, we needed both of us to bring our individual strengths to bear.

She produced a twenty-page document detailing every aspect of The Project in minute detail. It started with 'Get MOT for car' and ended with an exhaustive list of potential employers. Along the way, it took in accommodation, tax issues, health cover, residency and language. Each week had a list of issues that needed to be dealt with and crossed off before we could move on to the next stage. There was nothing it didn't cover.

We swithered over how much time it would take to find long-term accommodation in Venice. We thought one week would suffice, but decided that two would give us contingency. We booked ourselves into a holiday flat we'd previously stayed at in Dorsoduro.

A date was fixed for 3 March 2012 and one-way flights were booked to Venice. This gave us approximately three months to complete the sale of the flat, move all our possessions into storage at my cousin's house and to retrain as English teachers.

It seemed a reasonable amount of time . . .

Birmingham, they say, has more canals than Venice. Edinburgh, almost certainly, has more roadworks than Naples. Sighthill is seven miles from Leith and the rush-hour drive takes forty-five minutes. Every month I spent thirty hours of my life inching to work, as the car bounced from pothole to pothole, along badly maintained roads. Every day I sat in traffic and imagined the petrol gauge moving inexorably from right to left, burning up money for the most banal of purposes. The reward for enduring this wretched journey was to arrive at work. It's a commute that brings out the worst in people. It brought out the worst in me.

On 23 December, however, the streets were relatively clear as the city wound down for the festive season. The opening movement of Bach's *Christmas Oratorio*, the Marseillaise of festive music, played on Radio 3. I turned the volume up to maximum. *'Jauchzet, frohlocket! Auf, preiset die Tage!'* – 'Rejoice, exult! Up, and praise the day!' Yes, indeed, because this was my last day at work and I would never have to make this journey again.

Leaving a job – even one you hate – is never as much fun as you think it's going to be. God knows, I've left enough of them. Most of my friends had already finished for Christmas and my farewell email generated numerous 'out of office' messages, so my mood was downbeat. Cards, presents, much shaking of hands and good wishes. I had a final modestly boozy lunch with a handful of friends at a rather grim pub that people only seemed to go to for leaving drinks.

I'm not going to bang on about the banking industry. Suffice to say that your prejudices about it are probably correct. The prerequisite of a successful company is that it needs to be run for the benefit of customers, employees and shareholders. Lloyds Banking Group, manifestly, was not working for any of them. If it were a football team, fans would have started chanting 'You don't know what you're doing' some time ago. But that wasn't the point. The job might have been horrible, but the people were a good bunch. Nice people who deserved better than this.

Time to go. I slipped my presents and my Swansea City FC mug into a box, and left the office for the last time.

My Swansea City mug was over twenty years old and had been a trusty companion since my student days, travelling with me through Holland, Germany, Switzerland, Italy and Scotland. Two hours later the bag containing my presents tore through and dropped a bottle of wine on top of the mug, cracking it irreparably. It felt as symbolic as Prospero breaking his staff.

There was no time to celebrate being out of work. The next day we drove to South Wales to spend Christmas with my parents for the first time in years. We arrived home to find a letter from our solicitor stating that missives were concluded and we had now, effectively, sold our flat.

We'd not been the best of homeowners. I had ignored a slowly dripping tap for three years, until the day – Christmas Day, to be precise – when it refused to turn off at all. A broken light socket with an exposed live wire a few inches above head height remained in place for eighteen months. The task of affixing pigeon spikes – which involved balancing on a chair, on a narrow balcony, sixty feet above the ground – was one I entrusted to my then seventy-year-old father. I have never been the most practical of men.

We had well and truly burned our boats now. If we were planning on coming back, it would have made sense to hang on to the flat, even though we'd make a loss on renting it out. However, we'd also decided that – should The Project fail – we probably wouldn't return to Edinburgh. It had been twenty years and it felt like time to move on.

We hoped that, at a stroke, the sale would remove all sorts of work and potential difficulties from Caroline's project plan. It was dispiriting to find that the net effect was to shorten a twenty-page document by a single sheet. It simplified things and added a decent sum to the war chest, but we had well and truly reached the point of no return.

In 1990, I considered Gary Moore's *Still Got the Blues* to be the greatest rock-guitar album of all time. I hadn't played a track from it since 1992. And yet, I could hardly bear to get rid of it. Twenty years ago, it had been important to me. If it was discarded, a little of my past would go with it. And this applied to hundreds of CDs, hundreds of books.

As part of downsizing, everything in the flat was mentally labelled as Stuff We Need, Stuff We Might Need In The Future and Stuff To Be Got Rid Of. Furniture was designated as Sell or Store.

We undertook a purge of our books. Classics which were available free as ebooks could go to the charity shop. There were those that we'd never got round to reading and probably never would; and those that, realistically, were never going to be read again. There were shelves and shelves of cookery books, too many of which were used for a single recipe and nothing else. We cut them down to six.

I came across Roger Protz's *300 Beers You Must Try Before You Die!* It may have been a fortieth birthday present. A flick through revealed a solitary Italian brew, Nastro Azzurro, a gardening beer best described as 'mostly harmless'. There wasn't going to be much need for it in Venice. Not without regret, I put it on the Stuff To Be Got Rid Of pile.

Clearing out my wardrobe revealed my old motorcycle jacket and helmet, kept for nostalgic reasons long after I'd sold the bike. It was time for them to go. I was delighted to find a smart Paul Smith shirt, in immaculate condition, but – upon trying it on – it appeared to have shrunk dramatically over the years. A black patterned shirt with silver buttons and collar tips reminded me of a time when I thought that was a sharp look for an evening out. It was a period of my life coincidentally known as 'The Single Years'.

We'd managed to accumulate a substantial number of paintings. Nothing, unfortunately, that was likely to make us a huge amount of money if sold; but art that we liked, or was important to us. Most would need to be stored. Once they'd been taken down, the walls of the flat looked like somebody had gone berserk with a nail gun. The future owners, we hoped, would understand. There were artworks that we seemed to have bought by mistake, that had never been hung, that could go to the charity shops.

A nice German lady bought half a dozen IKEA 'Billy' bookcases off us. I couldn't remember how the hell the removal men managed to get them upstairs in the first place, so each one had to be taken apart to get them into the lift. At least the lift was working for once; and the nice German lady came prepared with an electric screwdriver. The spare room became a sea of orphaned books. Why, if we had got rid of so much, did it now look as if we had more than we had had in the first place?

The period between Christmas and New Year was intense. I've never liked New Year. As a kid, it means only one thing: Christmas is over, back to school. As an adult, it's even worse – you're going back to work and probably starting the year with a hangover. Lights and decorations come down, and we return to the cold, the dark and the rain until spring. Or, if you happen to live in Edinburgh, we just return to the cold, the dark and the rain.

Our previous Hogmanay had been a miserable one. I recalled standing on our balcony and watching the final trails of the fireworks at midnight, reflecting on a year blighted by the fear of losing our jobs. The feeling had been of utter helplessness and hopelessness, of being trapped in a grotesque, soul-crushing game against people who could appoint the referee and change the rules whenever they felt like it. And there had been worse, much worse: my sister, I had learned, was terribly ill.

Twelve months had now passed. It turned out that there had always been a way to win: simply to refuse to play. For the first time in years, we were entering the New Year happy and excited about the months ahead. We were in control of events instead of at their mercy and everything seemed possible.

We passed a pleasant Hogmanay with friends. Strong drink was consumed in modest quantities. We got home at a sensible time, and I went to bed with a cup of tea and an improving book. Next morning we woke, hangover free, ready for the day and year ahead, and congratulated ourselves for being middle-aged.

The holidays, even in Scotland, were now officially over. I had a number of tasks of varying degrees of importance to crack on with: the essential (pre-course TEFL exercises), the fun (browsing the internet for flats in Venice and seeing what was on at the opera) and the tedious-but-really-needing-to-be-done (arranging van hire).

I set to the TEFL prep. The language school where we were to take an intensive one-month course had supplied us with a list of background reading and preparatory exercises. To my chagrin they seemed to demonstrate that I did not actually have the ability to speak English at all. There were five days left until the course started and I felt I could sort that out by then. A vague melancholy was settling over me and I couldn't understand why. It was a general feeling of discontent, an unsettling anxiety that I was unable to shake. I didn't know what to do with myself, so I pottered about brewing cups of tea, stared outside at a hurricane blowing through Leith, grumpily channel-surfed between Radio 3 and 4, and got under Caroline's feet.

And then it hit me. It was the day that I would normally be back at work. Subconsciously I was expecting to be in the office and I was feeling guilty about not being there. I'd only been at the bank for seven and a half years and spent seven of those complaining about it; yet I was worried that the global financial system would go into meltdown if I wasn't there personally to sort it out. I put my TEFL exercises down. Van hire would have to wait until tomorrow. I logged on to the La Fenice website instead . . .

I graduated nearly thirty years ago, but every few months I get nightmares such as this:

It's the end of my final year at university. I have been to no lectures at all. I have completed no assignments. I haven't done a scrap of work on my project. Today, my finals begin and I have done no revision. I am going to fail my exams and ruin the rest of my life . . .

I am frequently trouserless in these dreams as well, but that's another story. I'd got away with it once and never again, I thought, would I have to study formally for any sort of qualification.

Except that now that's what we both had to do. TEFL training had started. And let no one tell you that this is easy. You want me to stand up and deliver a lecture to a roomful of people? No problem. Would you like me to sing to a roomful of people? I'd be delighted. Hell, if strong drink has been consumed you'd have a job stopping me! But teaching? That suddenly seemed like another matter altogether.

After the first hour, I started to worry if I could do it.

After two hours, I was certain that I couldn't do it.

After three hours, the thought struck me that we had given up our jobs and sold our home and so we were bloody well going to have to find a way of doing it.

Neither of us had collapsed in uncontrollable tears after the first day, so that was a positive sign. We were yet to be let loose on actual, proper, money-paying foreign students. Perhaps they would be kind to us.

We were an eclectic bunch on the course. Two women from Slovakia and Argentina whose knowledge of English grammar shamed the rest of us. A young musician from Paris. A number of army personnel, there to improve their teaching skills prior to training members of the security forces in Afghanistan. A man who had been attacked by a polar bear. We felt embarrassingly normal by comparison.

We had been warned about the amount of work that would be involved, but I had refused to believe it. How difficult could it be? Yet I have never worked so hard in my life as I did during that month.

Upon returning home, I would prepare a basic meal, before hammering away at lesson plans and essays until the small hours. The television remained switched off. So did the radio. Our regular 'No Booze January' meant we were denied the consolation of a restorative G&T. We lived an austere life of monastic asceticism.

But, in all honesty, I enjoyed that month enormously. It changed my perspectives. Initially I'd thought it would be a useful qualification to have in case I couldn't get a job doing anything else. By the end I found myself looking forward to putting it into practice. Maybe, all those years ago, I'd taken a wrong step with IT and this was something I should always have done. I was excited by the thought of making a living from teaching.

We ate, slept and breathed TEFL for four exhausting weeks; and then we found ourselves with teaching certificates. They were CELTAs and not PGCEs, but it had taken a lot of hard work to get that far.

For those who might be considering this: don't think that this is something you'll just be able to do. You won't. Don't believe it's something that you can't fail. You can, and the experience of watching someone floundering in front of a class is a horrible one. Don't let anybody tell you it's 'not proper teaching'. It's proper teaching to those who are going to pay you money, and you owe it to them to treat it with seriousness and professionalism. Clear your diary and set aside a quiet month. You cannot do this and maintain a social life. Well you could, but I'm a grumpy bugger without my sleep and I'm too old to be burning the candle at both ends any more.

It was hard to say goodbye to everyone on that final Friday night. They were a genuinely nice, interesting bunch of people, there for very different reasons. We had looked out for each other and had a lot of good times along the way. I wondered where we would end up and if we would see each other again.

I spoke to one of our tutors, over farewell drinks, about our plans to move to Italy. She told me that there was work there, and finding it would not be a problem. 'There is one thing . . . if you're in Italy you will need to teach children.'

I can't remember if I choked on my beer, or merely blinked. That was one thing I had never considered. Teaching children. I looked across the table to where Caroline was laughing and joking with some of the other students.

I decided to keep this nugget of information to myself. More than that, I did my best to forget it.

Everything seemed very real and ominously close now. We were to leave home in under a month and had less than two weeks to pack. More importantly I still had nearly 2000 CDs to deal with. It wasn't practical to transport the whole lot to Venice and we were not likely to be renting a place with sufficient space to store them anyway. I decided to rip them to my laptop. They might be in less-than-perfect-quality sound, but it would be better than nothing.

I should have given it about a year. Instead I left it until the final couple of weeks.

Compromises had to be made. What had to come with us? Beethoven, Brahms, Berlioz (almost everyone that starts with a 'B'). As much Bach as physically possible. Everything by Wagner. Puccini. The Beatles, Jethro Tull and Hawkwind. How our neighbours would love us, I thought.

It was an interesting journey through my musical past. Philip Glass's *Einstein on the Beach*, in which a man chants '12341234123412341234' for two and a half hours, made the cut. A set of ten austere string quartets by Peter Maxwell

Philip Gwynne Jones

Davies might have repaid long-term investigation, but there wasn't time. Sorry Max.

And then there was Mahler. I had five different recordings of his sixth symphony. I couldn't remember buying them all. I certainly wasn't convinced I'd listened to them all. And not only is it not my favourite symphony, it's not even my favourite Mahler symphony. How had I managed to acquire five?

I'd made it as far as 'M' and Wagner was still to come, where rows upon rows of CDs and box sets and multiple recordings stretched into the distance like the rainbow bridge to Valhalla.

It was a long week.

We'd been regulars at the Italian Cultural Institute in Edinburgh for years, as we attempted to get to grips with the Italian language. We'd settled into a consistent pattern of study over the years, namely:

1. Return from holiday mortified by lack of ability in Italian.
2. Book language course with best of intentions.
3. Give up after five weeks.
4. Go on holiday.
5. Repeat from 1.

I wouldn't recommend this to everyone, but the amount of repetition over the years meant that some of the language had sunk in, and in our final year we managed to knuckle down more than we had before.

As well as language classes, the Institute hosted cultural activities, one of which was linked to Pellegrino Artusi, a nineteenth-century Florentine gentleman, famous today for his work *La scienza in cucina e l'arte di mangiare bene* (The Science of Cooking and the Art of Eating Well). It was completed in 1891, just twenty years after the unification of Italy, and he is sometimes credited with establishing a national Italian cuisine. The Institute held a cookery competition to mark the centenary of his death and celebrate the republication of his great work. I thought I could take time off from working on The Project to have some fun.

I never used to be able to cook. In the years between leaving home for university and meeting Caroline I had managed to exist happily on a diet of sandwiches. And then the time came when Caroline was working a serious amount of overtime and it occurred to me that, perhaps, it would be better if she were not to arrive home exhausted to find me sprawled on the sofa, glass of wine in hand, and nothing prepared for dinner.

I needed to learn to cook, but I didn't know how to boil an egg. It would be an exaggeration to say that Nigel Slater's *Kitchen Diaries* saved our marriage, but it might well have saved my life. I became obsessed with cooking. Caroline realised something was up when, two weeks into my crash course with Nigel, she asked me if there was anything I'd like her to get from the market and I suggested a hare or a brace of pigeons. I'm still not great at boiled eggs, though.

A cookery competition – better still, an Italian cookery competition – sounded right up my street.

The rules were that all dishes would be taken from Artusi's book, be cooked in advance and be judged on the night of the Institute's celebratory party. This presented some problems: hot dishes wouldn't be practical and anything prepared needed to be transported by bus over the rattly old streets of Edinburgh and still look appetising by the end of the journey.

Pastries and desserts have never been my thing, so this narrowed my options. There were always *crostini*, but ... well, come now, *crostini* are more assembling than cooking, surely? No one was going to win a cookery competition with *crostini*.

I decided on Artusi's *Pane di Fegato*. Literally, a 'liver bread', part meat loaf, part pâté.

I chopped up some calves' liver and gently fried it in a not-insubstantial amount of butter. I added some chicken livers, a healthy slug of Marsala and more butter. I seasoned with salt and pepper and added breadcrumbs to absorb the juices.

I blitzed the mixture to a fine texture in the food processor. I added some eggs, parmesan, stock and a little more Marsala; rechecked the seasoning; and tipped the lot into a loaf tin where I cooked it in a bain-marie for approximately forty-five minutes before turning it out.

I took an organic chicken carcass, covered it with water, and simmered it for two hours, before reducing down the resulting stock to an intensely flavoured broth. Once cooled, I put it in the fridge for a few hours until it began to solidify into aspic.

I added a glaze to the loaf and then took four thin slices from an orange and laid them on top, before finishing with another glaze.

I made it twice, to be sure of what I was doing. It took a hell of a long time and cost a packet, but it was worth every minute. The texture was light and crumbly, the flavour surprisingly delicate. It looked utterly professional. It demonstrated technical ability in any number of culinary skills.

The winner was a bloke who made *crostini*.

Chapter 3

We were closer to leaving, and that meant saying goodbye to people.

It had been another busy day, and I had a rehearsal that same evening with the Edinburgh Bach Choir, with whom I'd been singing for a few years. Look, I said, I've got a ton of work to complete, I'm going to need every spare hour I can find and I could do without going to practice tonight. And I realised I was making excuses, because it was going to be my last evening with them.

Caroline persuaded me to go. I hadn't looked over my scores since Christmas – there hadn't been time and my heart hadn't been in it. But it would be the right thing to go, for one last time.

I hadn't planned to make any big announcement and thought I'd discreetly slip away after saying goodbye to those I knew best. It didn't work out that way. During the break our secretary stood up to read the usual notices about rehearsals and upcoming concerts and, to my genuine surprise, added 'Tonight we have some exciting but sad news, as Philip from the bass section is leaving us to move to Venice with his wife.' Applause, cries of surprise and I stood up to thank everyone. I would never get used to this sort of thing.

Handshakes, hugs and good wishes. Our conductor said they'd miss me and asked if there was any chance of arranging an exchange visit with a Venetian choir. I said I'd do my best to arrange the Monteverdi Vespers in St Mark's. I'm still not sure if he thought I was serious.

Caroline was already in bed when I got home. I gave her a hug and said I was going to sit up for a bit. I poured myself a large glass of wine, and sat on the sofa and cried as I listened to some Bach.

It was difficult saying goodbye to people and there was more of this to come. It didn't get any easier. But that was fine. Because this was never going to be a pain-free exercise. We both knew that we would have to give things up. We looked at what it would involve and still decided we wanted to do this. In a strange way, we found the seemingly never-ending round of goodbyes so draining and upsetting that it gave us confidence we were doing the right thing.

The choir wasn't important enough for me to put the move on hold. It was something that had only occupied me for a couple of hours a week. But I had loved those years with them and enjoyed their company, and it saddened me that I would probably never see them again.

The Biggest Casserole in the World sat on a kitchen unit, silently mocking me as I stood, helpless, in the face of its sheer immensity.

I hate packing.

I am rubbish at it. Caroline has quite the knack and packs away with millimetric precision. I am not like that. I gazed at the Biggest Casserole in the World in the manner of the ape creatures staring at the monolith at the start of Kubrick's *2001*.

'Do we need this?'

'It's Le Creuset.'

'Yes, but we've never used it, have we?'

'I did, once. Before we met. It was the only thing that could hold a whole chicken.'

'So we've not used it since at least 1998 then?'

'No, but it was expensive. And it's Le Creuset.'

I was never going to win this one. I'd already got away with labelling one box as 'Misc. Chinese thingies' so I didn't feel like pushing my luck.

I held the huge, circular lid in front of me, wondering if I could pass for Captain America. I found a box roughly the right size and packed it away. Never mind a whole chicken, this thing could have housed an entire free-range family. I taped it up, labelled it as 'Fragile' and then wondered why.

I manoeuvred it into position where it sat, tacitly asserting its authority over the other boxes of kitchen equipment. One day, oh yes, one day, I promised myself, we would cook the Biggest Chicken Casserole in the World.

Neither of us come from a big family, and our few relations are scattered around the country from Scunthorpe to Pembroke, from the Midlands to Hampshire, which has made it difficult to keep in touch as much as we'd like.

I may not have many relatives, but I'm lucky with the ones that I do have. I've always been close to my two cousins, since the days when we were kids playing on the beach in South

Wales. Both of them now live in Hampshire. Both are teachers, and were polite enough not to laugh out loud when I told them of my proposed change in career.

Cathy now lives in the New Forest with her husband Paul, who, like me, had chosen the career path of computer programmer with aspirations to musical immortality on the side. Zoe, their younger daughter, was about to start teacher training at university and she was going to get my car. Paul was even luckier. He was getting custody of my salmon-pink Hank Marvin signature Fender Stratocaster. I had yet to think of a suitable bribe for Cathy but one, I was sure, would turn up.

She told me they had plenty of loft space, a garage and some empty outbuildings where we could store everything. It sounded ideal. The only catch was we'd need to transport it all across country.

I'd done something similar many years ago, when I'd driven a van from Holland to Aberdeen. I'd been in my mid-twenties and didn't have more than my stereo, an electric guitar, a few suitcases of clothes and my ex-girlfriend's bicycle. I still managed to get it wrong and ran out of petrol as I was passing through customs, to the delight of officials who assumed they were on the point of arresting the most inept smuggler ever.

This was different. Despite the downsizing, this involved transporting a lifetime's possessions across the country. If I ever meet the lovely man who designed the £25 trolley from B&Q, I will buy him a large drink. Without his wonderful invention, I have no idea how we would have got the van packed in one day. It took the two of us seven hours. It was a disturbing thought that 95 per cent of everything we owned was sitting outside, overnight, in a convenient drive-away form. In Leith.

We went to the opera that night. Humperdinck's *Hansel und Gretel*, influenced by Wagner, but minus any of that Wagnerian *Sturm und Drang* and soul-searching. Or length, for which, at that moment, I was grateful. Conducting the premiere, Richard Strauss described it as 'a masterpiece of the first rank'. Richard Strauss, however, had not spent a day loading his worldly possessions into a van and was not facing a four-hundred-mile drive in the morning. This was one of those rare occasions when I was less than enthusiastic at the prospect of a night at the opera. Crawling into bed and sleeping for twelve hours seemed a much better option.

Many years ago, at primary school in South Wales, *Hansel und Gretel* had been the first operatic music I heard. There was a pleasing symmetry to this being our last evening with Scottish Opera. It was a nostalgic evening to end on, with some fine playing and singing from a number of company stalwarts. Again, it was saying goodbye to friends and it wasn't getting any easier.

After a long, but mercifully uneventful, drive we arrived in the New Forest and by midday on Saturday I was standing in the middle of a half-empty van. The boxes had been cleared and were ready to go up to the loft. All that remained was to move the furniture into one of the outbuildings and we would be done. With five of us working we were nearly finished, and it'd only taken an hour. It was a fine, sunny day – rain was forecast for the afternoon but by that time, I thought, we'd be enjoying a late lunch in the pub.

Those few minutes of delusion would be the high point of the day.

The outbuilding was hidden at the back of a large garden, concealed by trees and bushes. You sort of stumbled across it like in the last few minutes of *The Blair Witch Project*.

We opened the door and looked inside. It was not quite as empty as we'd been led to believe. It was packed full, a galli-maufry of dusty, cobwebbed furniture and unidentifiable household objects. I stared at the interior, blinked, and turned to look at Cathy.

She shrugged. 'Sorry. It's been a while since I've been in here.'

We had two chests of drawers, a large wooden table, a quadruple wardrobe and a bed frame in the van. This wasn't a case of moving a few things out of the way – there was no way in hell we were going to fit everything in.

A plan was needed. Cathy, Caroline and Zoe would clear out everything that could be classified as rubbish. Paul and I would bring the furniture down. When the van was cleared, we'd chuck all the junk in the back and drive it to the dump. As we carried a wardrobe through a forest, in the rain, I began to suspect that the pub was not in our immediate future.

Eventually, we cleared the van and managed to squeeze the furniture into the shed. Paul and I retired to the kitchen to put the kettle on. My uncle Colin arrived to offer moral support. The loveliest and funniest of men, I have always thought he was the reason why the phrase 'mildly eccentric' was invented. He was a man who had been told to 'sod off' by Dylan Thomas, and who once made my breakfast explode. He told us that the outbuilding contained a few pieces of wood that he'd been whittling away at over the years, and hoped we wouldn't get rid of those.

After a chat over tea and a biscuit, the situation no longer seemed quite so bad. I wandered outside to see how the girls were getting on . . .

Somehow, I managed to maintain my grip on my cup of tea. The van, half-empty fifteen minutes ago, was jam-packed full of crap: cardboard boxes, tins of paint, flower pots, sheets of plastic, bicycles, scooters, garden furniture, a bed, a cooker hood and half of something which might once have been a chaise longue. Uncle Colin's carvings, I assumed, were somewhere in the middle. There was not an inch of space left. Over the course of thirty-six hours we had packed the van, unpacked it and now we were going to have to drive it to a dump and unload it all over again.

Cathy came over to me, saw the expression in my eyes, and looked genuinely concerned.

'Are you OK with this, Phil? Really?'

I gulped, and tried to keep the hysteria out of my voice. 'Hey, it's a van full of shite, Cathy, why wouldn't I be OK with it?'

I checked my watch. We had an hour and twenty minutes until the dump closed. Paul and I hauled our weary bodies into the van and set off.

I'd been living in hope that this was going to be a landfill and we could shovel out the contents and head off. Oh no. This was one of those facilities with a separate skip for every conceivable type of waste. I picked up a random, soggy cardboard box and made my way towards one marked 'Household

Waste' when a Polish gentleman in a waxed jacket stopped me, examined the contents and informed me 'Electrical cable – metals – over there on left. Tins of paint – paint recycling opposite. Plant pots – household waste. Cardboard box – papers – over there. Plastics – next to cardboard.' Half dazed, I stumbled from skip to skip. Another worker at the paints recycling bin sent me away for bringing the wrong type of paint.

Paul's face wore the haunted expression of a man who had taken a day's holiday to help us, and who had realised that this wouldn't be happening to him if he'd just pretended his boss wouldn't give him the time off. Occasionally his lips moved, repeating the words 'remember the Stratocaster' like a mantra.

I grabbed a Fisons bag full to the brim with tins of paint that looked as if they might be special enough for the special paints bin. I dragged it over, opened the lid and tipped the lot in, realising too late that the bag was also half full of peat. I closed the lid in a hurry and beat a hasty retreat.

We had a stroke of luck as the Polish chap abandoned his post, either to go for a cup of tea or to avoid the sight of two grown men crying. We seized the opportunity of the 'Household Waste' bin being at our mercy and, with Herculean effort, the Van Full of Shite was cleared. We jumped in and headed for home before he could return to identify any rogue items in his skip.

In our absence the girls had stashed away our paintings in a secure, concealed cellar (a nice touch, even if it did bring to mind images of fleeing Nazi war criminals). That left one final push – forty-odd boxes to be taken up to the loft. We evolved an efficient production-line: Cathy would drag a box from the pile and pass it to me. I would push it up the ladder to Zoe – the only one young and strong enough to haul it through the gap – who would slide it to Caroline and on to Paul (who was the only one who knew which areas of the floor were load bearing and which areas would allow a box full of Swansea City football programmes to crash through with lethal force onto the occupants of the room below).

And we were done. It felt like we should open a bottle of champagne but none of us would have had the strength to get the cork out. It had been a bugger of a tough day, but nobody had fallen out or been reduced to tears. There had been no casualties beyond Uncle Colin's carvings. As we relaxed over fish and chips and a modest amount of wine, I reflected that everybody had got something out of this. We had our free storage. Zoe had the car. Paul had the Stratocaster. And Cathy . . .?

Cathy had the Biggest Casserole in the World!

There were now just three days to go before leaving Edinburgh. The flat was not quite an empty shell, but felt cold and depressing. A small spray of flowers in a mug sat atop an upturned plastic crate that served as a coffee table. We were sleeping on an inflatable mattress and cooking was reduced to whatever could be warmed up in the oven or microwave as we had no pans left. Laughing at the Biggest Casserole in the World no longer seemed so funny.

It wasn't all Dickensian deprivation and misery. We still had a lot of wine left, which needed to be drunk before leaving. And there was the strange case of the cocktail cabinet, or, strictly speaking, the cocktail cardboard box; a nostalgic look back at our drinking history. A tiny swirl of green fluid in a bottle was a reminder of the short-lived, and possibly ill-advised, absinthe revival of the late 1990s. There was a half-glass of Pimm's left, as there had been since 1998. I had vague memories of cooking with kirsch and Strega; mainly because I couldn't imagine drinking either of them. There was a bottle of ouzo. Neither of us likes ouzo. I hadn't touched the stuff since a party in Swansea in 1988. Yet here was a near-full bottle that neither of us could remember buying. What was it doing? Loath though we were to dispose of anything vaguely alcoholic and not actually poisonous, it went down the sink.

The penultimate day came. All that remained was to clear out and clean the flat, pack our luggage and collect our euros. A final dinner with friends. And then that would be that.

It didn't work out that way.

I sound more Welsh when I'm angry and I stood at the foreign exchange desk in Sainsbury's sounding Very Welsh Indeed. Not the full Michael Sheen, but the Welshometer was creeping into the red. I'd driven forty minutes across town to pick up some euros and now the young man behind the counter was telling me that my payment hadn't cleared and he couldn't give me anything. I told him I'd rung an hour earlier to check and had been told everything was ready. He apologised, but he couldn't do anything. I drove home. The moment I stepped through the door the phone rang. It was, of course, Sainsbury's. Everything was cleared now. I drove all the way back. The lad handed over my euros. I drove home again.

This had wasted a whole morning when we had no time to waste. It was obvious we'd underestimated the amount of work left to do. A hell of a lot of stuff remained to be taken to the dump or to the charity shop, the place needed a good clean and we ('we' in this case meaning 'Caroline', as I'm not to be trusted with delicate operations like this) hadn't been able to start packing yet.

I spent the afternoon vacuuming and cleaning floors. I cleaned and polished the windows before turning my attention to the oven, which I hadn't touched since before Christmas. The interior resembled something from *The Quatermass Experiment*. I attacked it with a noxious chemical goo, emblazoned with all sorts of dire warnings, which rendered down the unpleasantness into a thick, fatty black sludge. I had always known that there would be times when the glamour and excitement of The Project would fade. This was one of them.

It was time for our last Italian class, following which everyone headed off for a bite to eat and a few glasses of wine. It was our final big farewell meal and bittersweet as always.

We returned home, feeling happier. The boys next door had bought us a very nice bottle of Riesling as a moving-out present and we thought a glass or two before bed would be just the thing. Caroline went to check her email, in case there was something that needed to be looked at urgently.

There was a message from the owner of the flat we were to be renting in Italy. The harsh Venetian winter had caused the pipes to burst in the flat upstairs and, as a result of the flooding, it was in no fit state to be occupied.

It was four days until we flew out, and we no longer had anywhere to stay.

Caroline got up at 2.30 a.m. in order to start packing. I was going to need a proper night's rest if I was to drive for seven hours so she let me sleep on, but I passed an uneasy night nonetheless.

There was no time to think about the flat, or lack of one, in Venice. Caroline packed and repacked, then repacked again. I shuttled back and forth, taking what remained in the flat down to the car for a final run to the charity shop or to throw into the building's two communal bins. I filled one and half of the other, and started to worry if I might be done for tipping. We thought we'd taken almost everything we owned down to Hampshire but, somehow, there was still so much of it left.

I came across a small box containing a cuckoo clock, a Christmas present I had bought for my late grandmother while I was working in Switzerland. She had loved it. And yet, we were never likely to hang a cuckoo clock on our wall. It broke my heart, but it had to go.

Everything seemed more difficult than it ought to have been. I had a bag of kitchen knives. Charity shops, in Leith at least, do not take bags full of knives, and I'd been told to take them to the police station. Along I went, pressed the intercom and informed them that I was standing outside with a bag of knives that I'd like them to dispose of. Two young policemen came out. They seemed confused. I held up the bag – slowly – through which sharp objects were already ripping holes, and explained the situation. They told me that they only disposed of weapons and these didn't count. I pointed out a wicked six-inch blade that, I imagined, might be used quite successfully for that purpose, but as it wasn't a samurai sword or a machete they wouldn't take it. One of them tried to be helpful and told me that I should take them to recycling or put them in the bin. I looked around me. A skip was conveniently, enticingly, placed on the street twenty yards away. It was tempting. I shook my head. I was not putting a bag of knives into a skip in Leith. I drove out to the recycling depot, and chucked them in the metals bin.

Caroline was still repacking, but we could see an end to it. I loaded the car. Amazingly, everything that now met the definition of 'essential' fitted in. Every square inch of free space was filled. Not a chink of light could be seen in the rear-view mirror. This probably counted as overloading. It almost certainly wasn't safe. If I had to do an emergency stop a painting balanced on a stack of boxes was likely to hurtle forward and decapitate me.

We should have left the flat at ten o'clock. It was now two in the afternoon. Caroline had been working, non-stop, for twelve hours. I needed to drive to Sheffield for the first stop on our farewell tour. Both of us were shattered. This had been the grimmest day so far but surely the worst had to be over.

'Let's go to Venice,' I said, and we left Edinburgh, and Scotland, for perhaps the last time.

Our morale improved over the next few days, due to the company of friends and heroic quantities of wine. There was the not inconsiderable problem of the uninhabitable flat to sort out. Our landlady, resident in San Francisco, told us with admirable Californian sangfroid that the situation was 'just a real bummer for everyone'. We pointed out that, for us, this was rather more than 'just a bummer', it was in fact 'a considerable bummer', and given that we were now of no fixed abode perhaps she might like to organise somewhere else for us to stay. Eventually she came back to us, having had a rethink. After speaking with her rep in Venice, they'd come to the conclusion that – although the flat would need redecorating at some point – it would be in a fit state for us to move into. I was past caring what a 'fit state' meant. If it had a roof, it would do.

Caroline repacked again and managed to reduce the number of cases to what we hoped would be a manageable number. Ten. I thought it was time for me to make the great gesture and told her that I was prepared to forego taking my opera cloak with me. She told me it had failed to make the cut four days previously.

In Hampshire, we stayed with my cousin Susie and her husband Justin, who would be driving us to the airport. Cathy and Paul arrived to say cheerio and to pick up the car. I handed over the documentation and suggested to Paul that I should run through some of its quirks such as the non-cancelling indicators and the intermittent central locking. I showed him how the satnav worked and the travel computer.

'I can't help noticing', he said, 'that all the instructions seem to be in Italian.'

'Yes, I changed all the language settings when I got the car. I thought it would be a good way to practise.'

'Right. Any idea how you switch them back?'

'Erm, I can't remember. Sorry. Anyway, Zoe speaks Italian . . . doesn't she?'

'Well . . . I guess she's going to learn.'

Susie and Justin drove us to Gatwick in an efficiently packed and extremely snug Zafira; and then it was hugs and goodbyes. We watched their car disappear, hauled our bags onto trolleys and realised we were now on our own.

Six months ago we had jobs, a flat and a car, and now – for the first time in our adult lives – we no longer possessed a key to anything. If our luggage failed to arrive we would be left with the clothes we were standing up in. The time to be nervous was long past. There wasn't any apprehension now, just a sense of absolute freedom.

I tried to watch and remember every minute of the final approach to Marco Polo. It felt like coming home. It wasn't, of course, and the following months would show us how much we had to learn; but I was aware that whenever we made this flight in the future it would never be the same.

A water taxi from the airport to Venice was expensive but the only way to transport so much luggage at once, and it was, admittedly, a special way to arrive. As the boat entered the Grand Canal I imagined I was Lord Byron arriving in the city for the first time, although Byron probably didn't have a laptop case on his knee with a copy of *Doctor Who Magazine* poking out. The driver dropped us at Campo San Barnaba, which was the nearest we were able to get to our flat on Calle Lunga. It was only a few hundred yards away, but a few hundred yards with ten heavy bags between two of us was not going to be possible in one go, so Caroline headed off to get the keys while I watched the luggage.

47

Giuseppe, the guy who looked after the flat, was out of town until later that evening, so he'd made arrangements to leave the keys with a Signor Colussi who lived a few doors down.

Caroline returned after fifteen minutes. Signor Colussi did not appear to be at home. Not to worry, we'd made good time and it was warm enough to sit outside, so we dragged our luggage to a nearby bar and ordered some drinks.

Time passed, and I thought I should go and check what was going on. Signor Colussi did not answer his door, but his neighbour saw me ringing and informed me that she thought he was out of town at the moment.

Still, there was no reason to worry, Giuseppe would be back in the evening. I'd give him a call on his *cellulare* and see what time he was due back.

There was no answer.

We ordered some more drinks, but it was starting to get chilly and no longer felt like ice-cold Peroni weather. We gave it another half-hour and then Caroline remembered she had Giuseppe's address so she could go and bang on his door and see if he was back.

I drew my coat around myself. It was properly cold and getting dark now. I did not know of any hotels in the area or how we were going to be able to look for one while trying to cope with ten heavy bags. It would be fair to say that, by the time Caroline returned, I was in danger of working myself into A Bit Of A State.

Happily, she had found Mrs Giuseppe at home, where she had been all afternoon with a spare set of keys, and who thought it funny that we'd spent hours nursing our drinks in the cold when our nice warm flat was only a few hundred yards away.

It took three journeys to transport all our luggage. I hauled the last of the bags upstairs and looked around. There were a few areas where paint had crumbled from the ceiling; but we'd finally made it. It was dry, it was warm and at that moment it was the best damn flat in the whole of Venice.

Chapter 4

Nothing felt real in those first few weeks.

We quickly realised we were not on holiday. On previous visits we had kidded ourselves that renting an apartment and cooking at home was the same as being a local. It was nothing like it. Our first trip to the Billa supermarket on the Zattere brought it home. It's one thing shopping for food as a tourist. It's another trying to find household staples – bleach, washing-up liquid, kitchen towel, toilet rolls – when nothing is the same as back home; when you find yourself without the safety net of reassuring brand names, or the instinctive knowledge of what something should cost.

Everything was different. The radio was different. The television was different. The newspapers were different. Who the hell were all these people being referred to on the news anyway? We should have been prepared for all this, but it still came as a bit of a shock.

There was also the issue of language. Well-meaning Venetians noticed that our Italian was less than perfect and would, after initial pleasantries, speak to us in English. This led to strange and frustrating conversations where both parties would obstinately plough ahead in the other's native tongue, as if not wanting to admit defeat. It made us feel like visitors; as if we didn't properly belong. But that's what we were – tourists who weren't going home.

After the past few months, it would have been pleasant to relax a little, to be on holiday for a while, but there was no time. We'd assumed two weeks would be plenty of time to find a long-term place to stay. Short-term rentals, even outside peak season, can be expensive and the clock had started ticking. The longer we spent in a holiday apartment, the more money – money that we could ill afford to waste – was burning up.

Yet there were those lovely moments of strolling through Dorsoduro and realising that we were not going home. We lived here now and had all the time in the world to enjoy it.

Day 1: Bits of ceiling plopped onto my head as I shaved. I looked up and noticed that another bit had crumbled away, and shook some paint and plaster fragments from my shaving brush. The flat looked nice enough at first glance but, if you raised your eyes from the horizontal, it became obvious that our landlady and Giuseppe were going to have more than a little redecoration to do.

There was work to crack on with and plenty of it, but we felt we could spare one day off. It was a cold, blustery day, with the winter sun breaking through. Venice was quiet, a genuine pleasure to walk around. We bought some fish from a stall in Campo Santa Margherita: *merluzzi*. I had no idea what they were, but they sounded exotic.

Fish on a Tuesday was a luxury for us, the fishmongers of Sighthill being notable by their absence. We picked up some basic white wine, coming in at just under two euros a litre.

Home for lunch, and Caroline put together a list of flats to visit. We strolled from Dorsoduro to Piazza San Marco. There were a few lines of tourists but they seemed outnumbered by *extracomunitari* selling imitation Louis Vuitton bags, a few of whom were hurriedly packing their wares away, presumably at the approach of the police. Ten minutes later we saw two policemen walking across the square, bearing a big pile of Mr Vuitton's not-quite-finest.

I baked the *merluzzi* (which turned out to be nothing more exotic than cod) for dinner, along with some *cime di rapa*. Washed down with some budget prosecco and even-more-budget white wine, it all felt like a treat.

Day 2 and the state of the ceiling had not improved. Another piece of plaster dangled ominously from the ceiling, but I'd become a dab hand by now and positioned an empty pedal bin beneath, before prodding the offending piece so that it dropped into the receptacle instead of crashing to the floor and fragmenting into a thousand pieces. I was pleased with myself, all the more so when we went to the fish market and managed to discuss the subtle, but important, differences between two species of clam without too much confusion.

More importantly, it was a day of starting to grapple with red tape. The *Codice Fiscale* – or tax code – is, supposedly, the easiest piece of documentation to acquire, and so it proved. We arrived at the Agenzia delle Entrate (the revenue agency) and sat in a queue for ten minutes, until an affable gentleman checked our passports and gave us the required documents. All done and dusted, conducted in Italian, and he even chuckled politely at a feeble joke of mine. We were wondering what all the fuss was about regarding Italian bureaucracy.

The Resident's Certificate was a different matter. We needed proof of our savings (we forgot to bring that), of our health cover (in the post) and a translation of our marriage certificate (hadn't even thought of that), although the more obliging of the two women at the Ufficio Anagrafe (Register Office) suggested that the last one wasn't that important and we could pretend to be living in sin if it made our application easier. The less obliging of the two advised us to come back when we spoke Italian. Caroline had the presence of mind to ask them to write down everything we needed to bring next time, on a Post-it note. This would prove to be invaluable.

We found ourselves standing outside, shell-shocked. We'd thought we were prepared for everything and, all of a sudden, the most vital parts of The Project didn't seem to be possible at all. And it turned out we didn't really speak Italian.

This brought us down to earth like, well, a piece of soggy plaster dropping from a bathroom ceiling. But the Joneses do not give up and have a little cry in times of adversity. They seek solace in strong drink; and in the company of a beer and a view of the Giudecca canal on a sunny day, few problems seemed insurmountable.

I cooked risotto with *vongole* for dinner, as a Maria Callas compilation played in the background. I don't even like Callas that much; nevertheless, the whole experience felt stereotypically, but magnificently, Italian. Yes, I know she was Greek.

You don't have to do anything in Venice. It is enough just to be there. Our first weekend allowed us time off from the job of settling in to wander around and enjoy the city. It had been sunny for days, the skies a clear blue; still cold in the shade, but feeling as if it would be just a few more weeks until it was jackets instead of coats.

We bought a rabbit from a butcher's in Campo S. Margherita. He only had half of one left, but it must have been a fearsome beast in life. It would have been a brave fox that dared to meddle with it. Hell, I'd have been scared, looking at the size of the thing.

Vegetarian friends, please look away now. Nothing of interest remains in the next few paragraphs.

We weren't kitted out for fancy cooking and neither did we want to be buying lots of ingredients. So here is the simplest of recipes for 'Rabbit Jonesy-style'.

It came complete with (half) its offal, so I warmed some oil in a pan, flipped out the half of the brain and gently fried it (veggie chums, if you're still here, I did warn you, and it doesn't get any better). I finely chopped the kidneys, liver and tongue, and added them to the pan. I turned up the heat, added the rabbit pieces, and fried them until golden and crisp on the outside. Then I added the juice and zest of half a lemon, a few sprigs of rosemary, a healthy glug of white wine, and covered it for fifteen minutes.

Served with some *cavolo nero* and crusty bread, it was the tastiest rabbit dish I had ever cooked. It could have fed four; nevertheless, we had no problems scoffing the lot and the bones made for a fine stock.

Flat-hunting started in earnest on Monday morning. We found an apartment we liked, decided it was 90 per cent perfect and dithered while we pondered whether we could live with the other 10 per cent. Inevitably, by the time we made up our minds, it had gone.

Later that same day we saw a small flat tucked away in Castello; not ideal in terms of size or location and we suspected it might be prone to *acqua alta* (i.e. flooding) as well. It was reasonably priced, though, and – being on the ground floor – would allow us to get a cat. Our previous moggy had proved to be a disappointment, a crotchety bundle of bad humour. We still missed having one, and thought it would be nice to have a Venetian cat. We'd have somebody on whom to practise our Italian. That wasn't enough in itself to make the apartment a realistic possibility, but it was something to add to the list.

Dinner that evening was *pasta alla Norma*, only made with Venetian *bigoli* instead of spaghetti. I'd like to say this was a deliberate attempt at Venetian/Sicilian fusion cuisine, but no. We didn't have any spaghetti in the cupboard. Aubergines are happy to absorb as much olive oil as you care to throw at them (and I threw a lot at these) so it may not have been the healthiest of dishes, but it was pretty good.

A visit to the Co-op in Cannaregio had introduced us to the ninety-cent litre of wine. Previously we'd thought the *vino sfuso* concept (take along plastic bottle – chap behind counter fills it up from enormous vat for not-very-much-money-at-all) was as good as it got, but this was a whole step beyond. For ninety cents (or, in this case, sixty, as there was a sale on) you took home a litre of wine in a Tetra Pak.

How good could a ninety-cent litre of wine be? The answer is that – while it was unlikely to win any awards – it was better than something that price had any right to be.

I leave you to ponder the likely social effects of introducing the ninety-cent litre of wine into the UK. In Leith they'd probably have to introduce martial law.

If Venice is a fish (and it is, just look at it on a map), then Giudecca is the curved sliver of land beneath the underbelly; separated from the main island by the Giudecca canal. It's not a part of Venice we knew particularly well. We usually made a visit during Biennale time when the Welsh pavilion was housed in an ex-brewery on the island. Nowadays the brewery has been converted into luxury apartments, but one scuffed 'Cymru' sticker remains on the pavement as a reminder.

We were here to see a flat. This wasn't the area we most wanted to stay in and the flat was in a modern development, but it seemed worth checking out. Rents are cheaper here, but we'd have an increase in commuting time as we'd need a boat to get anywhere we were likely to be working.

The flat was better than we expected. Bigger than anywhere we'd seen so far (for that matter, it was bigger than anywhere we'd ever lived), it came complete with every mod con and an outside terrace. It faced the island of La Grazia on one side, and the church of the Redentore on the other. It was a lot of flat for the money. Yet it wasn't quite right. The view towards the Redentore was a lovely one, but interrupted by a number of uninspiring modern buildings. If – as we thought – we might only be able to stay for a year, then we needed to find somewhere exactly right. It sounds shallow, but we wanted to be looking at old things.

It was a possibility. It was a bright, sunny day but pleasantly cool in the quiet, shady streets; we took a stroll around.

Giudecca is home to a number of intriguingly abandoned churches: Santi Cosma e Damiano has been converted into that most banal of things, a 'business centre', which itself looks deserted. Le Convertite is a women's prison. The guidebooks can't seem to agree on what has become of Santa Croce – opinion is divided as to whether it's an old people's home or a prison. After being shouted at by some guards for daring to look inside the gates, we can now confirm to the world that it is, indeed, a prison. Either that or it's the toughest old people's home you're likely to find.

With no plans for the afternoon, we headed to Dorsoduro and took a long lunch outside on the balcony. The ninety-cent bottle of wine had now been usurped by the sixty-nine-cent litre from Billa. 'Clever Vino Bianco' (for so it was called) was just about white-wine-flavoured. But only just. It didn't need to be tried again.

We'd miscalculated how long it would take us to find a flat. I'd naively assumed we could sort it out within a week; two at the most. But we were starting to realise that Italy didn't work like that. The more places we saw, the more our ideas were firming up as to the kind of place we really wanted. This meant a place in the *centro storico* proper with somewhere to sit outside. Caroline had said this was non-negotiable. I could understand. We'd spent seven years in an apartment in Edinburgh with a balcony that we hardly used. The last attempt had been two summers ago when we had sat outside in winter coats, drinking Martinis, until we were driven inside by the horizontal rain.

We were still in temporary accommodation, but had needed to move out of the flat on Calle Lunga. We would have stayed if the option had been there, but the owner was no longer replying to our emails. In addition, I was getting tired of the increasing state of dilapidation. The ceiling seemed to have stabilised, but mould had started growing at an alarming rate on one of the walls and, while I didn't mind occasionally having to hoover up crumbling plasterwork, I drew the line at donning a biohazard suit and washing the surfaces with bleach.

The new temporary place in San Basilio, by contrast, felt bright, airy and clean; and I thought the structurally sound ceiling compensated for the lack of a balcony.

We'd never thought about living in San Marco and had hoped to find somewhere further from the madding crowd. Yet one of the properties we'd seen in the area seemed perfect, almost enough to risk making an offer without seeing the inside. We nevertheless disciplined ourselves to waiting a week until the owner was back in town.

We'd been warned that we should not be too enthusiastic when flat-hunting in Venice. People would be willing to negotiate – they'd be expecting to. So that's what we intended to do. We'd be cool about it and express mild interest, but nothing more.

Our good intentions lasted the time it took to climb up to the *altana* and see the view that extended over the *sestiere* of San Marco, past the campanile of Santo Stefano and over to the dome of the Salute. We looked at each other and nodded. We had to have this place. We'd just give the owner what she wanted. Hell, we'd give her more if need be. We tried not to babble too much as we spoke to her.

Dinner that night was Venetian-style calves' liver and onions, with a side dish of baked radicchio. The sixty-nine-cent 'Clever Vino Rosso' seemed better than the white but, given I was drinking it to celebrate a Welsh Grand Slam in the rugby, I wasn't in a position to give an objective opinion.

My mobile rang at 10.30 on Monday morning, sending me jumping a foot in the air. I checked the number and hastily stabbed the reply button. This could only be about the flat. We'd been fretting about it all weekend and were tetchy and on edge.

'Philip speaking . . . yes . . . yes . . . OK . . .'

Caroline, ashen-faced, leant on a kitchen unit for support.

'OK . . . yes . . . right . . .'

Caroline made frantic, worried 'What IS it?' gestures at me.

'OK . . . yes . . . I understand . . . yes . . .'

I gave her a thumbs-up.

W H E E E E E E E E E E E E E E E E E E E E E E E E E E HHHHHHHH!!!!!

'Yes . . . yes, that was my wife . . . yes, she *is* pleased.'

Neither of us had expected to get it but it seemed that the owner had, in principle, agreed. We needed to head down to the agency's office in San Marco to make a formal offer. It was a pleasant walk along the Zattere, despite the grey skies and light drizzle. Within minutes of turning into San Marco, the heavens opened with a crack of thunder. It took five minutes until one of my boots started leaking. After ten minutes, both of them were. As we crossed the bridge over to San Moisè we saw a mournful-looking group of tourists in a gondola, putting a brave face on what must have been a dispiriting experience.

Water poured in torrents from the waterspouts around St Mark's Basilica; the piazza itself near-empty as people sheltered in the arcades. It struck us that we were in no hurry and could make the most of the opportunity to pop into the Basilica. How extraordinary, what a privilege, to be able to just 'pop into' St Mark's in the same way as one might drop by a bookshop or newsagent.

It is the loveliest of buildings and yet previous visits had always been disappointing – sadly shuffling around, shoulder-to-shoulder, in the midst of great throngs of visitors. There never seemed to be any space, or silence, to appreciate it. Our first ever visit, on a freezing New Year's Day, had been to the soundtrack of Paul McCartney's 'Wonderful Christmastime' resounding across the piazza. On that afternoon – whether it was the time of year or the bad weather keeping people indoors – it was relatively quiet. In an ideal world I'd like the place to myself, to stretch out on the floor and gaze at the ceilings. But, given that's unlikely to happen, this was one of our better experiences there.

We went on to the agency to sign the initial documentation, although we would have to wait until the following Thursday for a formal agreement to be completed. It had been a good day, and even squelching home in some soggy socks failed to take the shine off it. I couldn't be bothered to cook so we headed off to Al Profeta for pizza. We even spent more than sixty-nine cents on wine.

The next step was to open a bank account.

A visit to the nearest branch involved a walk along the Zattere and crossing the Grand Canal via the Accademia

Bridge, leaving us time for a coffee in Campo Santo Stefano. In Edinburgh, it required a forty-five-minute drive from Leith to Sighthill. This took roughly the same amount of time but, as an experience, the similarities ended there.

Opening an account over here is a relatively straightforward process, although simplified for us by an Italian-Scottish friend who had kindly telephoned her branch to tell them that two Brits would be arriving at some point. They seemed to have been expecting us, everyone was very helpful and polite, and within twenty-four hours we had an account and a *bancomat* card. We had to sign about a dozen different forms, but compared to the Byzantine complexity of opening, say, an Irish bank account (a tortuous saga that took me three months while I was working on a six-month IT contract in Dublin), this was a walk in the park.

Incidentally, before opening a bank account, you need an Italian mobile phone as they won't give you access to online banking without one. And you can't get a mobile, even pay-as-you-go, unless you have a Codice Fiscale. There is, probably, a good reason for this.

Bit by bit, we were ticking off the most important items on Caroline's masterplan. We were now proud possessors of a flatteringly entitled 'Super Genius' account. I liked to think this ranked somewhere above the basic 'Quite Clever' account and that someday we might hope to upgrade to full 'Renaissance Man' status.

It took half the number of signatures to complete a year-long lease on our flat. It had been a stressful week. Every time the phone rang we assumed it was the agency ringing to tell us that the owner had changed her mind. But, in an official ceremony at their office, it was finally completed. Everything, again, was extremely formal in comparison to the UK. Sitting around four sides of a glass and chrome table in a modern office space, drinking minuscule espressos from chic little coffee cups, it felt akin to Reagan and Gorbachev signing the Reykjavik agreement.

There were a few more hoops to jump through. Our agent kept reminding us that our landlady was very nervous about the prospect. She seemed to be a nice woman, however, and I could understand her being twitchy about renting her lovely flat to two unemployed Brits. Our workaround, and something I'd thought might be our ace in the hole, was to offer twelve months rent up front. It still wasn't as easy as all that, as the process of transferring a large amount of money from a British account to an Italian one is laborious. I had hoped to turn up for the final meeting in a sharp suit and dark glasses, with a briefcase full of euros chained to my wrist, but Mario Monti's new government had made any cash transaction above one thousand euros illegal. The solution was to transfer the entire amount, over two days, in ten bite-sized chunks. Each one of those payments incurred a hefty charge. It reminded us why we loved banks so much.

It was difficult to get too wound up about it. Everything was signed, sealed and almost delivered. Within a week, the flat would be ours and we could start to believe that, yes, we really lived here.

Chapter 5

March 2012 is an odd month to look back on for all sorts of reasons; not least is that, for four weeks, we were of No Fixed Abode. The Italians struggle with that concept. On numerous occasions we were asked to supply a permanent address and the response to being told that we didn't have one was a look of baffled incomprehension. In Italy, you can't *not* have a permanent place to live. It isn't possible. If you're trying this yourself, make sure you've got an address in your home country that you can use for this sort of thing.

Finally, the day of the Big Move arrived. The distance between our holiday flat in Dorsoduro and our apartment in San Marco was about half a mile, as the crow flies. But half a mile as the crow flies, in Venice, can turn into five miles. Ten, if I was navigating. Confusingly, it could also become less than half a mile. Venice is no respecter of the laws of Euclidean geometry.

The move involved transporting ten back-achingly heavy bags over a number of bridges. Any route chosen had to minimise these. It took patience, time and planning of near-military precision to work it out. Needless to say, I had no part in it. We hauled as many cases as we could manage to the San Basilio stop and took the vaporetto to Zattere. Just one stop, but it was enough to cut out a bridge. We walked to Accademia and took the number 1 service to Sant'Angelo. After a short walk and a bridge of manageable dimensions, we were there. Straightforward enough and it only took three journeys. I still got lost twice.

No cooking was ever likely to happen that night. We enjoyed a pizza of modest quality and immodest price (ah yes, we were in San Marco now) before moving on for coffee and grappa at what turned out to be an excellent bar on the corner of the splendidly named Calle dei Assassini. The Street of the Assassins. That, I thought, would be a great location for a book . . .

What had started out as a 'blokes in pubs' conversation had become a pipe dream, then a fully fledged Project and now – *we'd done it*. Somehow, we'd actually done it. There was a huge amount of work still to do – health cover, residency, improving our Italian, *work* – but as we sat on the *altana* of our flat, watching the sun going down, the only thing that mattered was: we lived in Venice now.

If there was a drawback to the flat, it was the tiny kitchen. That didn't matter. I'd get used to it. One Saturday morning, Caroline returned from the market with something that was going to be a challenge.

Moeche: Venetian soft-shell crabs so delicate they can be fried and eaten whole. They're a delicacy in the UK, so much so that I'd only had them once before. She'd managed to bag a dozen for a bargain seven euros.

These were going to take some work. You can't just chuck them in the frying pan. First you have to give them a long soak in water to purge them. It's important that the little chaps are alive when you buy them, but these seemed inert. Nevertheless, immersion in the sink perked them up no end and some of the bigger ones were keen to explore the limits of their new environment. Perhaps a little too keen. I made sure I counted them all, in case I returned to find a couple had made a break for it. If left alone for too long they'll start eating each other. I was worried I'd return and find a single giant crab sitting there contentedly.

Next step (vegetarian friends, you know the drill by now) is to beat a few eggs in a bowl, with a sprinkling of salt, and immerse our crustacean chums in the mix. The theory is that little crabs are absolutely bonkers for raw egg and will eat and eat and eat until (and the theories are divided on this) they either painlessly eat themselves to death or fall into a deep sleep. At which point you dredge them in flour and into the pan they go.

Whatever the theory, none of them were moving either before or after entering the pan, which was a relief as I wasn't relishing the idea of prodding any escapees back into the hot oil. And were they worth it? With a healthy sprinkling of salt and lemon they were, without doubt, one of the most delicious things I'd ever eaten. If you get the chance, try them.

A gondola passed by our flat that same evening. The gondolier was singing 'O Sole Mio'. Seriously. It's not even a Venetian song (at least one Lega Nord politician has got very cross about this sort of thing) but, come on, we'd been in the flat for a week and now a gondolier had floated past singing

'O Sole Mio'. There may be a more archetypically Venetian experience but – short of finding oneself following a sinister red-cloaked dwarf through the foggy streets – I struggle to think of one.

We were settling in, and finally unpacked, after what seemed like months of living out of suitcases.

It was interesting to see what had made the trip and what hadn't. I had arrived with two dress shirts, a bow tie, a selection of cufflinks and a white silk scarf. I would have looked quite the chap about town but the accompanying dinner suit was back in the UK. I had the detachable pocket from my opera cloak, but not the cloak itself. The camera, we could only assume, was somewhere in Hampshire. My ancient Swansea City scarf had made it. It has enormous sentimental value (I explained to Caroline that the scarf was at Preston in 1981, which didn't have the expected impact) but it wasn't something I'd worn in over thirty years.

A shame about the camera, but the extra scarf I thought might be handy come the winter.

Venice is unique among Italian cities in being a Patriarchate, a distinction awarded to it in the fifteenth century in recognition of its power. These days, the title of Patriarch confers no particular privilege, but the position is a prestigious one – it supplied three popes within the twentieth century alone.

The seat had become vacant when the previous incumbent, Angelo Scola, was moved on to bigger and better things (Milan, that is, not Heaven). His replacement was Monsignor Francesco Moraglia, a man who arrived with a reputation for being strong on workers' rights, the condition of prisons, and the dignity and rights of refugees. Arriving by train, his cortege set off down the Grand Canal, stopping for prayers at the church of the Salute, and then off to St Mark's to celebrate Mass.

Whatever your religious convictions, his arrival was an impressive sight. Surrounded by gondolas and boats from seemingly every rowing club in the city, he was escorted by numerous police boats and outriders kitted out in helmets and body armour. Police outriders in Venice ride jet skis. I imagine that must be a fun job.

Bridges across the Grand Canal were temporarily shut (the public were moved away from the area directly above the Patriarch's gondola) and the canal had been closed to other traffic for the duration; although one vaporetto blithely continued on its way against the flow of the cortege, the driver cheerfully oblivious to the chorus of angry beeping from police boats and to any potential threat to his immortal soul.

We had no trouble finding a decent vantage point, which surprised us. It was more surprising to find ourselves following him into the half-empty Salute. Despite all the colour and spectacle, and the privilege of being there at a moment of history, the streets and bridges seemed no busier than normal. The *Gazzettino* reported twenty thousand were at Piazza San Marco to welcome him. I can only say that the crowds looked considerably more modest to us. Times are changing, perhaps, even in a city of over one hundred churches.

The city was full of music for Holy Week, and where better to start than with Giovanni Battista Pergolesi, one of those composers who is only widely remembered for a single iconic work. His *Stabat Mater*, commissioned as a piece for Good Friday in honour of the Virgin Mary, was written early in 1736. Admired greatly by, among others, J. S. Bach, it proved enduringly popular. Pergolesi never lived to enjoy its success. Within weeks of its completion, he was dead of tuberculosis. He was twenty-six years old.

A performance of his great work was held at the church of the Salute. The Santa Maria della Salute, to give it its full name, is one of Venice's 'Plague Churches'. It was commissioned as a plea for deliverance from the pestilence of 1630–1 that would ultimately kill a third of the city's population. The architect chosen was the twenty-six-year-old Baldassare Longhena, but buildings such as this don't get thrown up overnight, and he died at the ripe old age of eighty-two, five years before the building's consecration.

I like the Salute. In contrast to its Venetian baroque exterior, the octagonal interior feels clean, unfussy and spacious. There was a modest audience for the performance (a number of people dropped by for a quick pray and then went on their way), but it was a good one. The two singers were almost concealed, high up in the organ loft behind Longhena's great baroque altar. The opening phrase 'Stabat Mater Dolorosa' seemed to emerge from nowhere, to echo around the apse. Spine-tingling music and a fine way to spend an afternoon.

That evening we fixed our nameplate over our doorbell. It felt as if we should have cracked a bottle of prosecco over it.

The run-up to Easter brought back memories of my first experience of living and working in Italy. One evening, twenty years past, in my little village in the Colli Albani, I became aware of a lot of noise coming from the square behind my flat; I stuck my head out of the window to see what was going on. It turned out to be a fully fledged Passion Play, complete with a convincingly bloodied Christ dragging his cross through the streets, followed by a sizeable number of the residents. With eerie – and suitably apocalyptic – timing, the skies darkened, a colossal storm broke, and within minutes the streets were awash and lights flickered on and off throughout the town.

Easter, in Italy, feels different to the UK. Church attendances may be declining, but there is still the sense that it matters to many people.

We decided to attend Mass at St Mark's on the Thursday night. I wasn't convinced this was a good idea. Neither Caroline nor myself are Catholic, so was this not – at best – disrespectful? I was half expecting to be turned away at the side entrance to the Basilica. The church, however, was properly geared up for foreign visitors. The most significant parts of the Mass were prefaced by translations in four languages and it was stressed that only Roman Catholics should receive Communion. The Basilica was crowded but more people could have fitted in – we weren't denying one of the locals a place.

We managed to follow the service reasonably well (it's not all that different from the Anglican service) considering that we were constantly having to leap mentally between Latin, Italian and English. The evening service on Holy Thursday is more correctly known as the Mass of the Lord's Supper, a significant element of which is the Washing of Feet. In this instance, the Patriarch washed the feet of a number of children who were about to receive their first Communion. I was amused to see that many of them were 'dressing down' for the occasion – jeans and trainers under robes were common. The service concluded with the consecrated Host being taken to a side chapel in readiness for Good Friday Mass.

It was a powerful experience. The golden glow of the interior of the Basilica, the clouds of incense, the music from the (invisible) choir, the slow procession of the priests and, everywhere, those extraordinary mosaic images from the Bible. Religion with a capital 'R'.

We returned the following night for the Veneration of Relics. This doesn't have any liturgical significance as a service and so didn't attract the same number of people. It was a memorable evening, nonetheless.

The relics were brought out in solemn procession and placed along the iconostasis: a fragment of the Cross, a scrap of Christ's robe, a piece of the column from the Flagellation, two spines from the Crown of Thorns, one of the nails and part of the reed from which Christ, on the Cross, was offered vinegar. A small crystal vial set in an ornate golden reliquary was set upon the altar. It is said to contain blood from the spear wound. Readings were interspersed with music (beautifully sung antiphonal pieces from Palestrina, Monteverdi and Mozart); following which the relics were carried through the aisles of the Basilica.

Again, as an experience, it was undeniably powerful. As a piece of theatre it was extraordinary, reminding me of the Grail ceremony in Wagner's *Parsifal*. But I ask myself, how much of the emotional impact was due to its theatricality and music? Did I stand there genuinely believing that I was only feet away from the actual Blood of Christ? And that, for me at least, was too much of a leap of faith.

Fifty years ago, in *Venice*, Jan Morris wrote of attending the same service, of the same quasi-mystical experience, and of the mundane realities of everyday life that came crashing in upon leaving the Basilica. We emerged into a clear Venetian night with a perfect moon above Piazza San Marco and were assailed within seconds by a street hawker trying to sell us tat. Some things haven't changed.

Chapter 6

Intensive Italian lessons were now only a week away, and it felt like the end of the holidays. That week coincided with *La Settimana della Cultura* – Cultural Week – and so there was plenty to take our mind off going back to school.

Venice is not a cheap city but there are a healthy number of free events. One of these was a discussion on Richard Wagner and philosophy, hosted by the Wagner Society of Venice. The weather had been grey and wet all day, which seemed to have hit the audience numbers – just over twenty of us in a space that could have held a hundred. It was an interesting evening, and a ninety-minute lecture on Wagner and Schopenhauer was a useful workout for our Italian; if not of much practical use.

Wagner's list of dislikes, irritations and petty grievances was not a short one but he liked Italy, and Venice in particular. His first visit allowed him time to complete *Tristan und Isolde*, as well as serving as a place of refuge from his political enemies, his creditors and his wife Minna. His last visit ended in an argument with his wife, Cosima this time, who accused him of an affair with a Flower Maiden from *Parsifal*. Wagner, stung by her terrible (i.e. true) accusation, flew into a rage of, well, Wagnerian proportions, and worked himself into such a state he keeled over from a fatal heart attack.

His rooms, at Ca' Vendramin on the Grand Canal, are available to visit although, as the palazzo is now home to the city's casino, security is tight. You must book in advance, they are strict about numbers, you need to bring along some form of ID and you will probably be met at the entrance by Men with Guns. Entering the country seems easier and less intimidating.

If you are any sort of Wagnerite, this is a place you need to see. It's enormously interesting (there's a fine collection of memorabilia, including letters and scores) and humanises the old monster. He might have been as cuddly as a cactus, but seeing the bills for sending his gondolier out to buy champagne made me think he couldn't have been all bad. One day I hope to be able to do the same. At the moment, I'd be sending him to the supermarket for a sixty-nine-cent Tetra Pak of white wine, but one step at a time.

On a clear day, you can see the Alps from Fondamente Nove. We'd never managed to see them before until, on our way to catch a boat, we emerged from a *calle* and there they were. Proper mountains, not mere specks in the distance, but snow-capped peaks against an azure sky. A genuine wow moment, as if the Almighty had a flash of inspiration as to how he could make the most beautiful city in the world even lovelier.

We were in this part of town to catch a boat to the quarantine island of Lazzaretto Nuovo that once operated as a decontamination station for ships arriving from areas suspected of being a source of plague. The crew would stay for forty (*quaranta* – hence the English word 'quarantine') days, at which point – all being well – they were allowed to proceed to the city.

It served as a gunpowder store during the time of the Napoleonic and Austrian regimes and continued to be used by the Italian army until the 1970s. The island is now deserted, its guardians colonies of birds and some well-fed cats.

It's maintained by volunteers, who arrived on the same boat as ourselves. If you arrived unannounced (it's a request-only stop on the vaporetto) you'd find yourself unable to proceed any further than the locked gate on the jetty, with nothing to do except wait for the next boat passing in the opposite direction.

In the space of four months we had gone from working in a bank to strolling around a disused plague island. It seemed like progress. We passed a faded sign for the Ekos Club of Venice, the organisation that helps to run the place. I misread it as Eros Club and worried that we might be overdressed.

The guided tour was well worth it. The walls are painted with records of arriving ships, together with graffiti-style images of soldiers and boats. The buildings have been well restored considering the effort it must have taken (our guide described the island, pre-restoration, as 'a jungle').

Entrance, during Cultural Week, should have been free, but we were politely asked if we could make a small donation to the upkeep of the island, which seemed only fair. I took out my wallet to find that I had no small denominations. But the guy had been so nice, the tour had lasted an hour and they depend on voluntary donations; and so a free visit ended up costing twice as much as the normal charge.

This would normally have thrown me into a right old sulk, but the journey back on the boat snapped me out of it. The view was worth the entrance fee on its own.

La Settimana della Cultura was proving to be exhausting. A visit to the cloisters and refectory of San Salvador (now part of the Telecom Italia building); a talk on great figures in recent Venetian history at the Ateneo and one on Venetian serial killers at the Casinò; frequent visits to the Accademia and a hefty number of tours of historic sites. It was like the Edinburgh Festival with less rain.

Guided tours in Italy are not the same as in the UK. You must not expect a forty-five-minute stroll around prior to a cup of tea and a piece of cake in the café. These are proper workouts for the grey matter and there are few minutiae that will not be explored in detail. We attended a tour of the church of San Simeon Piccolo. After an hour we had progressed from the base of the steps to the main door, without any sign of going in. We bailed out and went for a drink. And an ice cream. Then back to the bar as I realised I'd left my bag there (it was still on the back of the chair – note to self, do not try this in Naples or Rome). We returned to the Scalzi bridge to find the crowd still outside the front door. They may very well be there still, no doubt thinking, *Let's just give it five minutes more, eh?*

An architectural tour of the buildings in the vicinity of San Bartolomeo was spoiled by an annoying bloke who kept interrupting the guide with unrelated questions. After forty-five minutes we had progressed perhaps a hundred yards and it was hard work, so we knocked this one on the head as well.

In the afternoon, we toured the Palazzo Grimani, only to find Annoying Bloke there again. This time he kept his powder dry for the first hour. There was no stopping him once he'd started, however, and progress around the last few rooms slowed to a glacial pace. A number of people looked pissed off, but nobody wanted to say anything, and – being foreign – we weren't the best people to speak up. Still, it's a fine building and we were pleased that we were able to understand the majority of an informative talk.

Buoyed by this, we stopped for a spritz and dropped by Ratti to buy a printer. At which point it became obvious that all we'd learned about the Grimanis and Salviati, of Sansovino and Palladio, was no use in an electrical shop in the absence of knowing the Italian for 'toner cartridge'; or 'USB cable'; or, indeed, 'printer'. It was just as well, then, that Italian lessons would begin shortly.

Let's take a pause, for a brief word on the spritz . . .

It is, perhaps, the ideal drink. On a hot day, the first half of a beer can seem like the best thing in the world. The second half can seem stale and warm (this is a general rule, and doesn't apply to those 'didn't even touch the sides' moments). A prosecco is fine, but not a drink that can be lingered over. The Negroni, magnificent as it is, is more of a special occasion drink for reasons of health and money. But *uno spritz al Campari* is bitter and refreshing to the last drop. For me, it has to be with Campari. I find Aperol too sweet and akin to alcoholic Irn-Bru. I like Cynar as much as I like most artichoke-based drinks. The slightly medicinal Select, said by some to be the most authentic, is stereotyped as being the preserve of old men; and while the past few years have seen me embrace the cardigan, I don't think there's a need to hurry things along any more than necessary.

I observed the swiftest of spritz-making masterclasses in the bar at the foot of the Accademia Bridge, where the ancient knowledge was being passed on to a young apprentice. I admired its almost Zen-like simplicity:

> Put ice cubes in glass
> Apply three-second burst from white-wine tap.
> Hold bottle of Campari upside down. Keep it there for three seconds.
> Fill up remaining space with three seconds' worth of sparkling water.
> Plop slice of lemon in.

The three-second rule seemed almost perfect so I gave it a go at home. Sadly, it doesn't really work without proper bar equipment to control the flow. Or maybe I needed a bigger glass. Nevertheless, whenever you see one being made, you can look for the count of three as a sign of quality control.

The *acqua alta* alarm sounded that evening.

Despite numerous visits over the years we'd never been in Venice at a time of high water (it can happen in summer, but it's most likely in autumn or spring) and then, one Saturday night, we heard some sirens go off as I was cooking dinner. For the new resident, the sound of the *acqua alta* alarm is like the four-minute warning – namely, you have no idea what it sounds like.

Caroline found the official website, where a sliding scale of alarms are detailed from 'you might want to take your wellies with you' to 'head for high ground immediately'. This was the lowest scale, but the man downstairs lowered the *paratia* into place. We had noticed that most Venetian houses had two brackets mounted outside the main door, into which the *paratia* – a solid metal barrier – could be dropped, with the intention of minimising the amount of water that floods into your property. We had no idea how effective these were.

In the months to come we would find ourselves in the wrong part of town at the wrong time, wading through all sorts of unpleasantness and hoping that the water would not reach top-of-welly level. But from the comfort of a second-floor flat, that first sound of the alarm was just a little bit exciting.

Nothing happened, beyond a couple of inches of water in Piazza San Marco, which felt anti-climactic. We were now signed up for warnings by SMS, but it seemed prudent to go and buy some welly boots as well.

Sunday morning involved a tour round the church of La Pietà, the church of the Ospedale della Pietà, the orphanage where Vivaldi taught and composed. Even in its day, this was more concert hall than church and nowadays it's difficult to have a look around without buying a ticket for a concert (which will, almost certainly, involve *The Four Seasons*). The Red Priest was dead long before the building was completed, but it seems he had some influence on the design: the acoustics, even for the spoken voice, are remarkable, and the sound of the choir and musicians of the orphanage – hidden from view behind screens in upstairs galleries – must have been wonderful. And beyond its musical significance, the church boasts a number of frescoed ceilings by Tiepolo.

It seemed like destiny that Annoying Bloke was in our party again. After five minutes our guide asked if anyone had any questions and our hearts sank as lunch receded into the distance. Time, however, was on our side as we only had an hour before the next group arrived, so try as he might (and he most certainly did) he was never quite able to get into his stride.

The rain kept us in the flat that afternoon, giving Caroline time to revise her Italian, as I prepared a calf's tongue with olives for dinner. Nicer than you might imagine.

Back-to-school day had arrived: the first day of Italian classes.

Caroline had spent the night, and much of the previous day, convincing herself that she spoke no Italian at all. I needed to judge the atmosphere with precision here. Should I go straight into full-on Supportive Hubby mode, bouncing along with smiles, hugs and 'It'll be all rights'; or was this a situation best played as if nothing untoward was happening? I decided this was not the morning to be Mister Life and Soul and chose the latter. It turned out to be the right choice and I awarded myself a bonus Hubby Point.

Enrolling was a painless and non-scary exercise. We'd already completed the online application; but there was a brief written test and interview to go through first, in order for them to be sure of our level. They claimed we were level B2 (or upper intermediate). I thought that was flattering but was happy to be flattered.

Our Italian wasn't all that bad. Unfortunately, it wasn't that great either and, given that we first started learning twenty years ago, it should have been better. I'd wasted my opportunity of working in Italy (it was an English-speaking office and most of my friends were expats); and successive attempts had got stuck in the pattern of starting evening classes with good intentions and dropping out after a few weeks.

The Great Printer Humiliation excepted, we could just about do everything we needed to; but not with ease or spontaneity. We needed to improve, so we had signed up for a three-month intensive course with the Istituto Venezia, based in Campo Santa Margherita in Dorsoduro; a pleasant twenty-minute stroll. Four hours a day, five days a week and everything in Italian – five years' worth of evening classes condensed into twelve weeks. This, surely, would set us right.

We were a cosmopolitan bunch in our class. Not everybody was there for the long haul but, at the start, there were three Swiss, two Russians, a Catalan, a Venezuelan, a Colombian, a Japanese, a Dutchwoman, an Englishwoman and a Scot. I was the only man, which turned out to be useful, as opportunities for gender-related conversation would otherwise have been limited. This set a pattern for the following three months, where male students were consistently outnumbered by women. I have no idea why.

A welcome party had been organised for us at the end of the first day's lessons and I talked to the Dutchwoman for a while. It turned out her husband worked for a company called Unisys, at which point I almost choked on my drink. Unisys were the suppliers of a financial payments system, the support of which had blighted my last three years with the bank. I'm sure he's a nice man and it wasn't his fault at all, so I told her nothing of the sleepless nights and days of horror it had caused me.

There was the matter of dealing with signing up to the health service. There are any number of books, blogs and articles that make Italian bureaucracy sound akin to one of the Circles of Hell about which Dante never got around to writing. If you're like us, you may have thought that these experiences were overwritten, playing on the worst of Italian stereotypes for comic effect. Or maybe you thought the party involved didn't have a good enough grasp of Italian or hadn't done their research properly. Then, one day, you'll run into a bureaucratic brick wall that seemingly has no way over, under or round. And like us, you'll regret ever having been such a smartarse.

We arrived at the confusingly titled ex-Ospedale Giustinian (confusingly titled because it still is an *ospedale*) to register with the Italian Health Service. We had our passports, our *Codici Fiscali*, our rental contract and bank account statements. Most importantly, we had our S1 forms, which stated that, in the event of us needing healthcare in Italy, the cost would be picked up by the UK NHS for a period of two years, or until such time as we entered the Italian Social Security System.

The receptionist gave us directions and the sign on the door indicated that, among other things, this was where foreigners should go to register. There was a short queue, so we took a ticket and sat down to wait.

It took ten minutes until our number was called and in we went. We'd scarcely begun to explain ourselves when the woman behind the *sportello* shook her head, grabbed a piece of paper with a phone number and address in Mestre, and told us to go away and try there. We attempted to explain that we'd come with our form S1, which needed to be registered here, and that it certified our healthcare would be covered by the UK. She didn't raise her head to look at it, but shrugged and said she'd never heard of such a form.

We found ourselves back on the wrong side of the door after, at most, thirty seconds. This was soul-destroying. This wasn't a question of language, it was sheer bloody-mindedness coupled with an unhealthy dose of not giving a toss. Neither of us had any faith that the office in Mestre would do anything other than send us back here. We didn't know what the hell to do.

And then something wonderful happened. The man who'd been sitting next to us asked, in English, how we'd got on. He looked genuinely concerned as we explained. His number was called so he asked us to wait while he had his appointment. Two minutes later he emerged, shaking his head. The *signora*, he apologised, seemed to have no interest in helping people. He took out his *cellulare*, dialled the Mestre office and explained the situation. He checked that they recognised the S1 and passed on all our details. He told us what we needed to take, made us an appointment for 8.30 on Monday morning and gave us a contact name.

We could have hugged him. We stammered a few words of thanks, but he smiled and said he was glad to help. As we left, he stopped at the main desk and politely, but firmly, remonstrated with the receptionist for not being sufficiently helpful to hapless *stranieri*.

The world may be run by tedious pen-pushers but, when you need one, there are still a few Lovely Blokes out there willing to lend a hand. Whoever and wherever you are, good sir, we salute you.

To Mestre, then, on the advice of the Saint of Ca' Giustinian. It should just have been a case of registering something that we were entitled to under European law, but it felt more like going into an exam or job interview. We weren't 100 per cent convinced that this would work and that we wouldn't be sent off somewhere else; and the long-term success of The Project couldn't be based on us never getting ill or needing any drugs again. Ever.

Happily nothing went wrong this time. A nice lady registered us in the system, assigned us a doctor and that was it. She even reminded us that we needed to update the address on our *Codici Fiscali* and confirmed that the documentation we now had was suitable proof of health cover when applying for residency. By ten o'clock we were on the train back to Venice and I started a mental list of Nice Ladies as a companion to the list of Lovely Blokes.

That left us with residency to deal with.

When you join the queue for the *sportello* at the Agency of Entreaties or the Office of the Anagraphs there are two things you should do: (1) take a book, (2) take a book.

We waited half an hour at the Agenzia delle Entrate, frustrating as we were only there to tell them we'd changed address. One of the blokes in the queue was obviously an old hand at this, as he'd worked out that he could stand outside having a ciggie in the sunshine and keep half an eye on the next ticket being called via the laser display board. I wondered if we should come prepared with a picnic in the event of requiring another visit.

They're a helpful bunch at the Agency and once we'd been called it was straightforward. Then it was on to the more forbidding Ufficio Anagrafe. If you tell a Venetian that you have an appointment there, they will respond with a dry laugh, a sad shake of the head, a sharp intake of breath, or a combination of all three. Whereas the Entreaties are based around the elegant cloisters of the ex-convent of Santo Stefano, the atmosphere inside the Anagrafe – despite being based in a palazzo on the Grand Canal – resembles the sort of grim Soviet police station to which you might be summoned after having been denounced.

Our number was called. It was the woman who had dealt with us last time, fortunately minus her scary colleague. More fortunately, we had a Post-it note with a list of all the requirements, in her handwriting. She seemed to be on our side this time, although baffled as to how we qualified for Italian healthcare. We had the certificates, but she didn't understand how we'd managed to get hold of them. She rang another office to check. Nobody was there, so we left with a promise that she'd call us the next day.

We were prepared for this to take a couple of days or, possibly, forever; but I got a call midway through Friday morning Italian class. I rushed outside to take it and was informed that all our documentation seemed to be in order and we should come along next Thursday to sign the forms. I got a round of applause when I reported this back to my classmates.

There was, inevitably, one more thing. They wanted two letters from the Institute confirming that we were studying there. I asked the secretary if she could provide them and said it was a request from the Anagrafe. She laughed, dryly, with a sad shake of the head and a sharp intake of breath.

We returned to our regular *sportello* the following week. Our *signora* had the documentation to hand and, after some more form filling, that seemed to be it. Her scary colleague had returned and occasionally interjected, striking fear into our hearts as she sent our lady off to check with a Higher Authority. Less than an hour later, our application for residency was formally in progress and it was a matter of verifying that we lived where we said we did for it to be approved.

Let me expand on that. They send someone round to the house in which you claim to be living so you have to give them a set of times when you will be there. This meant that I would need to stay at home, within earshot of the doorbell, for up to two weeks. At some point someone from the Comune would come a-knocking and . . . I didn't know what would happen after that. I assumed I needed to show them my passport. I wasn't sure if it would help to have drinks and snacks prepared.

We emerged from the Scuola Grande di San Rocco that evening, stiff of back and sore of bottom, after a two-and-a-half-hour presentation of a new book on the great Victorian art critic and social thinker John Ruskin, author of *The Stones of Venice*. We were among the hardy bunch who had survived the whole series of lectures, an initially healthy audience having dwindled to a handful over the course of the evening. It had been informative, enjoyable and – like Ruskin's great work itself – there'd also been a little too much of it.

Ruskin's attention to detail is staggering, obsessive even. There is scarcely a column, cornice or capital in St Mark's Basilica or the Ducal Palace that is not dissected and analysed in forensic detail. His reasons for this were simple – Venice, he thought, would either fall into ruin or, worse, be destroyed by restoration, and it was important to record what was there as best he could. Admirable, yes, heroic even; but it does not make the *Stones* an easy book to read.

He hated half the buildings in the city as much as he loved the other half. He considered the Gothic and the Byzantine to be the high points of architecture, but despised the baroque (the 'Grotesque Renaissance', as he calls it); while Palladio's Classicism drove him into a furious rage ('contemptible under every point of rational regard!').

Nevertheless, he needs to be read. It may not be necessary to read the whole book (indeed, without being as intelligent as the man himself, it may not be possible to read the whole thing) but he's certainly worth dipping into. When he dismisses a favourite building of yours with his curt (and frequently used) – 'of no interest' – you'll want to shout at him, 'Oh for God's sake, man, just *look* at the bloody thing, what do you mean it's "of no interest"?' But he's always erudite and informative, and – perhaps surprisingly – he can be waspishly funny and magnificently rude.

At the end of his days he seems to have felt ambivalent about his relationship with Venice, fearing that he had devoted too much time and energy to a city that he considered to be dead or dying; more of a museum than a functioning city. People are still debating that, over one hundred years after his death. Proof that the old place has some life in it yet.

It was past four in the morning. We'd had a disturbed night's sleep as someone with a loud boat and louder music had passed by twice, but we'd finally drifted off when . . .

BANG.

Not loud enough to scare us out of bed, but we were instantly awake and from somewhere came one hell of a banging and a crashing that shook the whole room.

My first thought, in my befuddled state, was that something was wrong with the washing machine, but that wouldn't make the whole building shake. And Caroline doesn't get out of bed to put the washing machine on at 4 a.m. I wondered if it might be one of the bigger cruise ships passing, but even they don't cause vibrations like this.

Caroline thought it was someone trying to break in. I didn't want this to be true because he would have had to have been a giant of a man to make the place shake like this and I wouldn't know what to do, other than slide money under the door in the hope he'd go away.

The thought hit me – *I suppose it could be an earthquake*. The banging and crashing had stopped, but the ceiling lights were swinging from side to side and the building was still juddering. Not frightening, but an unpleasant, uncomfortable feeling. I went to the window to take a look outside. Whenever an earthquake gets reported (and it's not that uncommon), the words *gente in strada* (people in the street) are used to indicate how serious it is. There was no one there and no sign of any disturbance. I heard the door slam downstairs. Presumably our neighbour was also checking if we needed to get out.

The vibrations died away. I went back to bed, but was unable to sleep. An hour later the aftershock hit – less noticeable this time, a gentle vibration and, again, the ceiling lights swayed. Caroline didn't wake and it has now been scientifically proven that my wife is capable of sleeping through an earthquake. The next day we found out that a quake of about 6 on the Richter scale had hit north of Bologna. The shock was felt as far away as Milan. Sadly, people had died. We tend to think that earthquakes happen in far-off places: it's easy to forget that Italy is one of the most seismically active countries in Europe.

The same thing happened two weeks later, this time in class. The room started shaking at about 9.10. Only a little but, as before, it induced an unsettling feeling. Alberto, our teacher, looked up at the light fittings swinging from the ceiling and shrugged. '*Ah, terremoto*.' Some of the students seemed perturbed but he joked that we should perhaps abandon the building and go for a coffee. We laughed and settled down for the lesson.

We felt the aftershock four hours later, a light shiver running through the building. A German lady in the class was visibly upset and got to her feet. She explained that she was in Rome when the 2009 quake nearly wiped L'Aquila from the map. She didn't want to sit down, there were only five minutes of the lesson left and so we called it a day.

There was no significant damage in Venice. A statue toppled over in the Papadopoli Gardens and slightly injured a passer-by, but that was the extent of it. But we were thinking the same thing – *If we can feel it here, what's happening a hundred miles away?* Later that day we found out: over a dozen dead and thousands more made homeless. And it doesn't matter if you're insured to the nines or that this is a prosperous Western country – the people of L'Aquila are still waiting to be properly rehoused a decade later.

Italian classes were occupying our mornings, so we suggested to the Anagrafe that the Comune could send someone round to verify our address during the afternoons of Monday, Wednesday or Friday.

They came round on Thursday morning.

A note had been left under the door asking me to telephone a Signor Blanco, as soon as possible, between the hours of 8.00 and 9.00. I rang the next day.

He wasn't there.

Caroline spent Friday afternoon on the *altana*. I spent it skulking and sulking indoors, waiting for the doorbell to ring.

It didn't.

I tried again on Monday. Signor Blanco was a man in a hurry who quickly cut off my garbled explanations in order to tell me that someone would come around at 2.30 that afternoon.

He arrived on time. We explained the situation (he chuckled and shook his head when we mentioned the Anagrafe) and he checked our passports. He told us that, in the eyes of the Italian state (and possibly the eyes of God), we were not married as we hadn't had a Catholic ceremony, but that made no difference to our status as residents. Our marriage status could be sorted out later (there are some minor financial/legal implications) if we got a translated certificate stamped and verified by a lawyer.

We shook hands and he headed out into the driving rain. Three days later a letter arrived saying the process was complete – as long as we paid one final (oh please let it be final) visit to the Anagrafe to sign for and collect our documentation. I was starting to miss the place anyway. Our *Tessere Sanitarie* had also arrived. We were officially allowed to be ill and had chipped a bit more from the mountain of bureaucracy.

We returned to the Anagrafe and greeted the *signora* with hugs, kisses and flowers. Not really, but given that she was, by now, the person we knew best in Venice, it felt as if we ought to. She handed over our documentation, pointed us in the direction of the *sportello* that dealt with the issuing of *Carte d'Identita*, and we made our farewells. Ten minutes later, we were standing outside with two spanking new identity cards certifying that we were Venetian residents, our photos stamped with two metal seals bearing the imprint of The Most Serene Republic. We were entitled to most of the rights of the Italian citizen, except the right to vote in parliamentary elections. We are entitled to vote in local and European elections. Even today, I still get a thrill from not voting for Silvio Berlusconi.

It had taken three months and been disheartening at times, but everything was finally complete. We had health cover, tax codes and official residency.

We stopped at a nearby bar to celebrate, thinking we had earned a drink. And not just any drink, but a Negroni. I don't know if you're familiar with the Negroni? Made of Campari, gin and red vermouth, it's a bit like being punched in the face but in a good way.

The *cameriera* brought us the bill and said she remembered us from a few weeks back, when – on account of my wearing a pin-striped jacket – she had mistaken me for a German. Caroline told her why we were so excited.

The *signora* looked taken aback. 'Show me,' she asked.

Caroline handed over her new *Carta d'Identita*.

She smiled, crumpled the bill in her hands, and knocked a not inconsiderable number of euros off the total. Next time, she explained, we should tell the owner that we were *residenti* and we would not have to pay the same as tourists.

There were many reasons for becoming residents: a sense of belonging, making a commitment to a new place, being strictly legal and above board, and entitlement to free entry to museums. Cheaper Negronis would be an unexpected and welcome bonus.

We never saw the same waitress again, however, and neither did we get any more discounted drinks.

Chapter 7

Everything had changed. We could at last say we lived here. We had a place to stay, we had all the necessary paperwork. There would be no more difficult visits to the Anagrafe.

I had thought that we should start looking for work as soon as we arrived. If we couldn't find a way of bringing money in through teaching, we needed to start thinking about alternatives as soon as possible.

Caroline insisted we took six months off and, of course, she was right. The process of relocation had been physically and emotionally exhausting; and the intensive Italian classes weren't leaving us much time to relax. It would have been absurdly difficult to job-hunt at the same time and attempting to hold down a job would have been impossible.

My concern was that we should be sending our CVs to prospective employers. Caroline pointed out that nobody would be interested in hearing from us in June; and sending out applications into the void, without getting any response, was going to work me into A State. And she was right again. If there was work to be found, it would be there in September. And if there wasn't, there was no point in making ourselves miserable before time. We'd be better able to deal with it if we relaxed and recharged for a few months.

We had a month of Italian classes left, but after that the summer would stretch ahead with no distractions. We would spend it on the *altana*, go to the beach, wander around town and make the most of every last *festa* or *sagra* – a local, often food-oriented festival – that came along. Ironically, having become residents, we found ourselves looking forward to being tourists again.

Ascension Day (or the *Festa della Sensa* in the Venetian dialect) celebrates the union of the Most Serene Republic with the sea; symbolised by the Doge throwing a gold ring into the Adriatic. There's a lack of doges these days, so the Mayor gets the job. Seemingly every rowing boat in Venice makes its way from San Marco to the Lido, where the ceremony takes place. The Mayor arrives on an impressive if slightly kitsch-looking boat recalling the great state barge, the *Bucintoro*, accompanied by the Patriarch. It's an impressive spectacle, although if you've seen one regatta you perhaps don't need to see them all.

Our very first Ascension Day would be spent at the Sant'Erasmo Festival of Artichokes. I was lukewarm about this. I mean, I like artichokes as much as the next man, but they've never struck me as the most festive of vegetables. The idea of spending Sunday at an artichoke festival made me feel that the rock-and-roll years were passing me by. Caroline was keen to go and, after I had dragged her along to a terrible *Orfeo ed Euridice* at the Teatro Malibran a few nights before, it was her turn to make decisions.

There was already a queue at the stop with thirty minutes to go. Neither of us was keen on the idea of standing in line for that long, so I decided there was time for a spritz. How many people were going to be getting on a boat to Sant'Erasmo on a Sunday afternoon?

Twenty-five minutes later, the answer was: a lot. Or, to be more precise, One Hell of a Lot. The queue snaked out of the stop onto the *fondamenta* and I realised I was going to be in big trouble if we didn't get on the boat. Somehow, everyone squished themselves on. I assumed that plenty of people would be getting off at Murano, but that turned out not to be the case. If anything, there was a net increase in the number. The crush eased, but only slightly, at the island of Vignole – it doesn't have much of a population, but with only one boat an hour it gets busy.

We reached Sant'Erasmo and enjoyed the luxury of breathing out again. The island serves as Venice's market garden. It's relatively featureless, although the trees and fields (and a handful of cars) are a novelty. It has a small population, but the houses look modern and expensive, and the place has a well-to-do air. The festival, based around the Fort of Maximilian, was a fifteen-minute walk along a straight, exposed track that would be unmerciful on a hot summer's day.

We arrived and there were artichokes. Lots of them. We wandered around to the strains of non-distressing live music, and settled down to a plate of artichokes three ways, along with the roughest five-euro bottle of red wine either of us could remember. I was forced to admit, however, that this had been a good idea. We took another stroll around and stopped at a stall selling excellent local wines, where the proprietors were good enough to let us fumble our way through a conversation in Italian. We left for home, many samples later, twenty euros lighter and, it seemed, members of a Venetian wine club.

We never heard another word from them. But it had been a more interesting afternoon than I might have thought.

Pottering about in the kitchen one day, I saw a guy laboriously moving a drumkit out of his front door and strapping it on to a trolley. My first thought was *Wow. Must be tough moving a drumkit around in this city.* My second thought was *Hurray! Our neighbour plays the drums!* Or something like that.

So, what were our neighbours like? Truth be told, we never really knew them. We occasionally saw the people downstairs, but they were often away for long periods and the flat lay empty for months at a time. The place next door was occupied by a French couple who spoke no Italian and put their rubbish out at the wrong time. I swapped *Buongiornos* with one of the guys in the street who wasn't allowed to smoke indoors and had to pop outside for a ciggie. He was an accountant based in Mestre. The population of our street, we were to find, was a transient one and people kept themselves to themselves. They included:

Artist Woman : occasionally seen at the end of the street, working on one of her big canvases. She seemed to be quite talented, but also disappeared for months at a time.

Declaiming Bloke: a strange fellow in a top-floor flat across the canal. He once kept the entire street awake into the small hours, reciting something, in English, possibly of a religious nature. People wandered into the street to find out where it was coming from, looked up, shook their heads and went back to bed assuming he couldn't keep it up much longer. They were wrong.

Party Animals: rarely, but occasionally a problem and twice held parties that went on until dawn. The third time one of the neighbours stuck his head out of the window and screamed abuse until they stopped.

Singers/Musicians: we had a high turnover – trumpeters, violinists, pianists, singers. Particularly singers. Some of them were first class. Others were, shall we say, 'enthusiastic'. There was something brilliant, however, about living somewhere where the neighbours were likely to burst into opera whenever the mood took them and it didn't matter if they weren't always the best in the world.

Action Movie Guy: a strange one. Every night, around 8 p.m., he put on a big action movie at maximum volume. Or possibly – given we never heard any dialogue – he put on a big action movie soundtrack. I became more familiar with the collected works of John Williams than I needed to be. This wasn't annoying in itself, as he was normally finished by 10 p.m., but the trouble was that he set off . . .

Screaming Children: people will tell you Venice is a 'cemetery town', inhabited by an ageing population. That has not been our experience. Kids played football in the streets near us (well, they did, but not for long ... in a contest between a canal and a ball there was only likely to be one winner) and there seemed to be any number of small children and babies in nearby flats. I felt for their parents. Just as they'd got the kids off to sleep and started to wonder if they might be able to relax with a glass of wine, Action Movie Guy would decide that what he wanted to hear, RIGHT NOW, was *Indiana Jones and the Temple of Doom* turned up to 11. With predictable consequences.

The one person we never heard a peep out of was the drummer.

It doesn't take long for the casual visitor to Venice to become acquainted with entrepreneurs of the street, eager to separate you from your money. During those first few months, we got better and better at identifying them. Here's a brief guide.

Bag Men: street vendors selling imitation Louis Vuitton bags. It's illegal, of course. Sometimes the police will have a crackdown and you see them packing up their wares and high-tailing it at speed, but, on the whole, nothing much gets done about them. They don't hassle you, which is nice, but laying out great rows of their wares leads to artificial corridors that make navigating narrow bridges and alleys more of a pain than it ought to be.

Crap Merchants: during the hours of daylight they attempt to sell you a rubbery ball with eyes and feet which, when dropped, splats itself into a gelatinous puddle before miraculously reconstituting itself. Over the course of our time here I have seen precisely two people stopping to buy these, as well as a tired-looking American tourist in a bar, trying – and failing – to replicate the effect for his son. Yet they're everywhere. After dark, the 'splatty' things are replaced with a sort of flashing gyrocopter device that can be fired into the air from a catapult before floating back to earth. The Crap Merchants are a pain in the arse. It doesn't matter if you are an ordinary couple going about your business, you will get hassled to buy a splatty rubber ball. And yet, the minute there's a bout of heavy rain, the Crap Merchants transform into Useful Merchants who will try and sell you umbrellas. Now that's not a bad idea, which leads me to wonder why they don't try and sell you useful stuff all the time?

Men with Roses: you used to see these guys in the UK. If you've stopped for a drink or a bite to eat, a man with a bunch of roses will approach and try and get you to buy one for your partner. He won't take no for an answer, the idea being that sooner or later you will feel like the worst husband in the world if you don't. Many people crack. I, however, am made of sterner stuff. At a restaurant one evening, a Man with a Rose stopped at our table and practically watched us eat. I thought he was going to pull up a chair at one point but, after I'd handed back for the third time the tired-looking bud he dropped on my side plate, he gave up and wandered off to the next table.

Buskers: a mixed bag. The chap who plays the lute on the Accademia Bridge in the evening is worth a euro of anyone's money. At the other extreme there was The Worst Busker in the World, a dapper elderly gentleman who sawed away tunelessly at an ancient violin on the Rio Terà Foscarini. He was unfailingly polite, and in his own strange way he was also worthy of the occasional euro. I haven't seen him for some months. I hope he's OK.

Those Who Don't Really Do Anything: for example, the man who dresses up as Charlie Chaplin and hangs around the environs of the Accademia Bridge. That's it. He doesn't do anything apart from dress up as Charlie Chaplin. He's a master of twirling his cane and standing in a vaguely Chaplinesque way, but that seems to be it. Presumably he must be making money, but it's not what you'd call an act.

The Petition Against Drugs: the most cryptic of all. If you have been to Venice you have almost certainly encountered them, a small group of people who hang around Campiello San Vidal or Campo San Salvador. You're asked if you speak English. If you answer yes, they ask you to sign a 'petition against drugs'. Most people will think that's a reasonable request and put their name down. At which point, having engaged you in conversation, they ask you for a donation; by which time you feel too embarrassed to say no, and walk on ten euros lighter.

A 'petition against drugs' is so vague as to be meaningless, and how much weight is a petition signed almost exclusively by foreigners supposed to carry? It's the equivalent of those spam emails against drink driving. If it's a scam, you don't want to part with ten euros; and even if it isn't, you'd be bankrupt within a month if you stopped and signed every time you were asked.

So what is it? Contrary to internet rumour, they're not going to pick your pockets while you sign. A Venetian acquaintance, while vague on the details, tells me that it is a legitimate fundraiser for a drug rehab charity, even if their method of dragging you in is rather sharp practice. On the last occasion, hard-headed businessman that he is, he suggested to them that it would make economic and social sense to legalise all drugs. He has not been hassled further.

It's almost impossible not to get accosted by them. We've tried switching to Italian before the moment of contact. We've tried not speaking at all. We've repeated 'signed, already' in both languages (and, in my case, through the medium of mime that I normally reserve for asking for the bill in restaurants) so many times that one of the girls now gives us a cheery wave and a *Ciao*. One Sunday, we walked past them without even an *Excuse Me* or a *Do you speak English?* Never mind the *Codice Fiscale*, never mind the ID card, never mind the *Tessera Sanitaria*. We felt, at last, that we truly belonged here. We had walked unaccosted past the Petition Against Drugs people.

Italy's contribution to world cinema is a great one. In the silent era, before German Expressionism, before the glory days of Soviet filmmaking, the Italians made technical advances that were years ahead of Hollywood. With *Cabiria*

(1914), they invented the 'epic' before Cecil B. DeMille and D. W. Griffith. In years to come, Fellini and Antonioni would make classics of European art cinema; and, in the genre movie, Mario Bava, Sergio Leone and Dario Argento would redefine and stretch the boundaries of the horror film, the Western and the thriller. It's an extraordinary body of work.

You would not know this from the state of Italian television.

My first encounter with it was during the 1994 World Cup. Among the grizzled old pros in the studio was a succession of glamorous female co-presenters, all of whom resembled Anita Ekberg in *La Dolce Vita*. This was an eye-opener after the UK's football coverage, where the only concession to glamour had been Jimmy Hill sporting an unusually colourful bow tie. Even with a shaky grasp of the language, it became obvious that their television wasn't so great and, in the intervening years, it had declined further. The blame for this can be laid at the door of Silvio Berlusconi, a man with a seemingly perfect record of taking things that were poor to begin with and making them worse.

What I'm leading up to is the fact that we don't have a television, and a computer has to suffice. This isn't a grand gesture on our part and I do not think our lives are richer for it, but what we've seen hasn't convinced us that it's worth the cost or the hassle of getting one up the stairs. I would suggest that every critic of the BBC spend one month with nothing to view except Italian television; following which the most rabid free-marketeer would be begging for the British licence fee to be doubled.

Enough of what's bad. What's good? Italian Radio 3 (RAI Tre), that's what! It's a mixture of UK Radio 3 and Radio 4, minus *The Archers*, but with extra weird things. A blend of news, drama, documentaries, classical music, jazz and general strangeness that took me a long time to work out. A programme about the film music of Ennio Morricone was suddenly interrupted, for no apparent reason, by a burst of Dire Straits and Pink Floyd. An entire Sunday night was given over to American minimalist composer Terry Riley (I managed ten minutes before Caroline made me turn it off). The week-day opera show appears to be hosted by Statler and Waldorf from *The Muppet Show*.

Much of the time it's enormously enjoyable and intelligent radio. I love it to bits.

Italian classes were leading us into the darker corners of the language.

You can make yourself understood with a grasp of the *presente*, the *passato prossimo*, the *imperfetto* and the *futuro*; and given that you can express the future using the *presente*, you don't even really need the *futuro*. The trouble is that, if you don't know the other tenses, you'll be at a loss when other people talk to you, or when you're reading a newspaper or book. If you're going to communicate politely, or with elegance, you need to engage with the *condizionale* and with the *congiuntivo* (the subjunctive).

This is difficult for English speakers to grasp. We don't often use the subjunctive and, when we do, we don't realise we're using it – think of expressions like 'Be that as it may' or 'If I were you'. But it's widespread in Italian for expressing opinion or doubt, so you need to familiarise yourself with four extra tenses.

Apparently it isn't widely used down south, which made me think in the future there might be mileage in a Naples Project.

On to the *passato remoto*. There is no English equivalent of this. If you went to the pub yesterday, or your great-great-great grandfather went to the pub in 1847, you express it in the same way. Not in Italian. There is a different tense for expressing what happened 'a long time ago'. A famous example would be Tosca's aria 'Vissi d'Arte' (I Have Lived for Art). You might not need to be able to use this in speech, but pick up a novel and you'll encounter it almost immediately.

I then discovered that in the south of the country it *is* used in everyday speech. Which put paid to the short-lived Naples Project.

The early stages of learning the language – listening to the radio, or to people talking in the street, is like playing bingo. As soon you hear a '*penso che*' or a '*credo che*' you brace yourself for an oncoming use of the subjunctive. At a lecture one evening by the artist Giuseppe Penone, I heard a *se* followed by a *congiuntivo* followed by a *condizionale*. I had to restrain myself from punching the air. A textbook example of the *periodo ipotetico*, sir, I salute you!

When you think you're getting a handle on this, you encounter something called the pleonastic '*non*'. Where '*non*' does not mean a negation, but something more subtle. Think of it as the difference between 'Italian is easier than I thought' and 'Italian is easier than I thought (not that I thought it was going to be hard anyway)'.

The Italians, bless them, have found a use for the word 'not', that (a) doesn't mean 'not', (b) doesn't need to be used, but (c) you need to be familiar with. At this point, like me, you put your head in your hands.

Or not.

Chapter 8

Ineeded to start singing again. Or, rather, Caroline realised I needed to start singing again. I missed it. We'd been to see a local choir, the Cantori Veneziani at the church of the Frari, and I'd checked them out on the internet. I was a little intimidated. These guys got to sing at the Frari, one of the most overwhelming interior spaces in Venice. I wasn't sure I'd be up to it. Or, to be precise, I wasn't sure my Italian would be up to it. This wasn't like buying fish from the market or a newspaper off a stand. This was going to involve making proper conversation and actually understanding what the *maestra* was saying to us.

I did nothing for a few weeks until Caroline pushed me into it. I turned up for an evening rehearsal at a school in Dorsoduro. Being British about things, I turned up fifteen minutes early to find that no one else was there. I wandered the downstairs corridors in silence, wondering where the hell I was supposed to be. It brought back memories of my first day at a new school. I was prepared to wait five minutes, give it up as a bad idea, and tell Caroline it was never going to work.

A few early arrivals turned up and took pity on me. I stumbled my way through my explanation, and the *maestra* shushed me. My Italian was fine, she said, and they were always happy to have new male voices. She handed over two scores.

The first was Leonard Bernstein's *Chichester Psalms*. That made me smile. There was something funny about travelling over a thousand miles to Italy to learn how to sing something in Hebrew. The other score was more obscure: Benedetto Marcello's *L'estro poetico-armonico*.

'I'm sorry,' I said. 'I've never heard of Benedetto Marcello.'

She asked where I lived. 'Off Campo Santo Stefano. Near the Conservatorio.'

She smiled. 'That would be the Conservatorio Benedetto Marcello.'

Oh well, things could only get better.

And they did. Everyone was kind and cheery and my status as the only Brit gave me curiosity value, especially when they found out our back story. They were a sociable bunch. Concerts and rehearsals would frequently end with a *rinfresco* of some kind. For the first time I was meeting Venetians in a social context. Over time, I'd recognise people in the street, just to say *Ciao*. It's not an exaggeration to say that the Cantori made the difference. They gave me the opportunity to sing in some of the most incredible buildings in Europe. They gave me a social life, friendship and help. For as long as I am able to sing with them, and beyond, that is something for which I will always be grateful.

I sat there, and listened, and sang, and wondered how my life had turned out like this. Ninety minutes later I left with a couple of scores under my arm. It had started to rain, but I didn't care. I skipped over the Accademia Bridge, the happiest man in Venice.

Summer was approaching, and Venice sweltered in the heat. Summer brought with it the 2012 European Football Championship. My free Euro 2012 supplement from *Repubblica* contained an article on every tournament and how Italy had performed. Some highs (the 1968 victory), some lows (the agonising last-minute goal that cost them the 2000 title), and the darkest moment of all: 2004. Referred to as *Il Biscotto*.

This sent me to the dictionary where I found, not entirely to my surprise, that a *biscotto* is a biscuit.

Was this a reference to a hitherto unknown performance-enhancing biscuit? I thought nothing more of it until the day after Italy drew with Croatia. Not the worst of results and the *Azzurri* were still favourites to go through, but suddenly biscuit fever was everywhere. The sports pages were full of it. Random Italian celebrities were being asked their opinion. Top motorcyclist Valentino Rossi confidently stated that he had no fear of the biscuit.

What the hell was this all about? It took some research, but I found that it referred to the aftermath of the final game of the first round of the 2004 tournament in which Sweden and Denmark drew 2–2: a result which sent both teams through at the expense of Italy. The two sides, the Italians claimed, had shared the last biscuit between them. It may have been a coincidence, but the Italians were convinced that both teams had fixed the result. Shockingly, they claimed, there may have been cheating. Ah, Mister Pot, I don't believe you've met Mister Kettle?

I felt like setting fire to my pile of Italian notes. Because memorising the entire Italian dictionary will not prepare you for, in the language of Dante and Petrarch, a biscuit that is not just a sodding biscuit but also 'a contrived result in a football match in which a mutually convenient result is played out'.

Italy had a must-win game against Ireland, but even if they beat them 100–0 they would still fail to go through if Spain and Croatia decided to remove a potentially awkward team from the latter stages of the competition by playing out a 2–2 draw.

Nobody knew if this was likely to happen or not but, in the hours leading up to the game, all of Italy was living in Fear of The Biscuit.

Italian classes were hard work in muggy, sauna-like conditions, and choir rehearsals weren't much better, despite being held in the evenings. Cramming fifty people in a classroom designed for thirty was always going to be a challenge in summer, and this one, so everybody said, was exceptionally hot.

The summer break was almost upon us, and an end-of-year party was scheduled to follow the final rehearsal. Every section was assigned food and drink to bring along on the last night:

Sopranos: Savoury dishes
Contraltos: Cakes and pastries
Tenors and Basses: Wine

The more observant among you may have noticed that the female sections of the choir had been asked to do some proper cooking, whereas the men were invited to stop by the shops and pick up a bottle on the way to rehearsal.

It didn't go unnoticed and, by an inevitable coincidence, the last rehearsal was the same night as the Italy–Ireland game that everyone had been getting into a state about.

Trouble ahead here, I thought.

Sure enough, I checked my email on Monday afternoon and found that one brave soul had suggested that if we rattled through the rehearsal quicker than usual we could get to the food and wine before kick-off. In fact, what if we sort of cancelled the rehearsal altogether and met up for a quick bite to eat between 8.00 and 8.30? Or, if somebody brought a television along, we could watch the match together?

The responses were swift and brutal, ranging from 'Tell you what, why don't you get there early enough to set the room up on your own and lay everything out in advance so we can throw this lovingly prepared food down our throats as quickly as possible?' to 'I have spent hours baking and if you think I'm going to spend the evening sitting in silence as the men gaze open-mouthed at a TV screen you have another think coming.' I'm translating as best I can, but you get the picture.

In short, the idea didn't really fly.

We rehearsed as normal and adjourned to the next room for the *conviviale*. The food was splendid, although would it have been the same if the men hadn't stopped to pick up some wine along the way? I think not.

It was a jolly evening. Italy beat Ireland, and Spain did the honourable thing against Croatia. The ghost of the biscuit of 2004 had been laid to rest, at least for this tournament. But I couldn't help thinking that it was just as well we'd broken up before the quarter-finals.

In addition to Italian classes, the Istituto Venezia did everything they could to entertain students after school, with guided tours, cookery classes and film nights. One thing in particular caught my eye: a visit to the Luigi Nono archive on Giudecca.

As we waited for a boat to Giudecca from the San Basilio stop, taking shelter from the sun in the shade of a nearby bar, the barman overheard our discussion and chipped in.

'Luigi Nono?' He smiled. 'Ah yes, I knew Luigi Nono!' We asked if he had any stories. He shrugged apologetically.

'Well, he was a good man. But I found his music quite difficult.'

'Difficult' is fair enough. Nevertheless, Nono is probably the greatest post-war Italian composer (and despite that giant Puccini-shaped shadow, a case could be made for him being the greatest of the twentieth century). During the 1950s he coined the phrase the 'Darmstadt School' to describe the work of himself, Pierre Boulez, Karlheinz Stockhausen and Bruno Maderna in attempting to create a new form of Western music; a form free of the nationalist associations that had been appropriated by the Third Reich. But Nono had little interest in creating purely abstract music – his works are inspired by architecture, literature and poetry, and are fiercely political. He died in 1990, but his archive was established in 1993 under the care of his widow.

The archive isn't far from the Palanca stop, housed in the cloisters of Sant'Eufemia, which also serve as artists' studios. Nuria Schoenberg Nono, Luigi's widow and Arnold Schoenberg's daughter, was there to greet us and show us around the archive. There are stage designs for his operas (or 'stage works' as he preferred to call them) and a complete set of scores; together with his private library, photographs, video and audio recordings. The photographs are a Who's Who of late twentieth-century music: the Darmstadt years show a handsome young Nono together with a glamorous, pipe-smoking Nuria, along with Boulez and an earnest-looking young Stockhausen. Most interesting are Renzo Piano's designs for *Prometeo*, premiered at the disused church of San Lorenzo and conducted by Claudio Abbado. Because, in a city where one can hear *The Four Seasons* every night of the week, the fact that three artists of the stature of Nono, Piano and Abbado staged such a work in the late twentieth century gives the lie to the cliché of the 'museum city'.

Nono's work is more popular in Germany than anywhere else these days – he never seems to have caught the imagination in Britain – but Nuria was pleased to hear that we had been able to see *Al Gran Sole Carico d'Amore* at the Edinburgh Festival, some years back.

I chatted with her about Nono's interest in architecture and his friendship with the great Venetian architect Carlo Scarpa. She asked if we still lived in Edinburgh and I explained how we'd moved to Venice, after leaving our jobs in IT. She smiled. Ah, the archive is always having trouble with their *informatica* – the machines are old, the network is slow, some of the applications no longer work.

I agreed. It's always the same with IT, isn't it? Something becomes obsolete as soon as it's out of the box. But if I could be of use, I'd be happy to help in any way.

She smiled and thanked me. We had to leave, so I had no idea if she was being nice, or if I should turn up for work on Monday morning.

As we left to make our way back to the *centro storico*, I realised that I had just passed ten minutes discussing IT strategy with Arnold Schoenberg's daughter. This is still the coolest and the nerdiest thing I have ever done in my life.

More traditional Italian opera took us to Verona in early July for a night at the Roman Arena. It was a toss-up between *Aida* and *Turandot* and – given that the latter was only on in August, when we could expect it to be even hotter – *Aida* won. Anyway, it's surely the quintessential 'stadium opera' and, if we were only going the once, we wanted to have the full experience.

The bus from Verona railway station to our hotel didn't take us through the nicest part of town and by the time we arrived – on a busy street thick with traffic fumes – I was starting to regret ever leaving Venice. But as we walked into town that evening, I realised that I'd done it a disservice: the town centre, the views across the river Adige and the pink marbled streets are all lovely.

A friend at the Istituto had recommended a place to eat, Al Bersagliere, which turned out to be one of those rare places where you want to eat absolutely everything on the menu. It's unusual for us to feel up to the whole *antipasti-primi-secondi* experience, but this time we thought we had to give it a go. We split a starter of polenta with *soppressa*, *lardo* and cheese; moved on to an awesome risotto with Amarone; and then Caroline had a veal escalope in a white wine sauce, while I had a fillet of beef that could be cut with a fork. I had room for a *diplomatico* (a *pan d'oro* with caramel) for dessert. I was on such a roll, I considered saying 'Bring the menu back my good man and let's start again from the beginning, eh?'

Time was getting on, so I went to pay the bill. I noticed a series of photographs behind the counter showing the owner in the company of various people. I assumed they were celebrities but I didn't recognise any of them until I did a double-take . . .

'Isn't that the Archbishop of Canterbury?' I said.

The owner beamed, '*Sì!* Mr Williams! He is my friend!'

The two of them had been at a function in Rome, organised by the Pope, and the then-Archbishop had given him his official invite as a souvenir. There they were, shaking hands, a demob-happy Rowan Williams looking happier than he had in years. I wondered why we never got invited to those sorts of parties. I hope we'll return one day for another splendid meal, and that next time we'll see a picture of our genial host with the Dalai Lama.

On to the opera. We passed a number of bars along the way, already packed in readiness for the Italy–Germany semi-final of Euro 2012. We took our seats. The production was a restaging of the classic one from 1913 and the sets looked as traditional as one could wish for. The arena slowly filled, the orchestra took their seats and the opera began.

The strains of the overture faded away. The singers moved forward. Almost silent. The drama was about to begin . . .

W W W W W HHH O O O O O O O O O O A A A A A A A A HHHHH!

Italy, presumably, had scored, as every bar in Verona erupted in joy.

This set the tone for the next couple of hours. There was the occasional WHOOOOAAAAHHHH but never quite enough to suggest that they'd scored again. And then there came a sudden cacophony of BEEEEPs from scooters, joining in with the WHOOOAAAAAAHHHHs and, as I checked my watch, I realised that it was full time. They must have won. The traditional post-match celebration of riding around on *motorini* and BEEEEPing had begun.

The third act wasn't able to compete.

And the opera itself? Well, seeing a production of this age makes you understand why staged opera had to change. There was a cast of hundreds and it was often beautiful to look at; but any sense of drama was lost in the spectacle and the acting never got beyond the old-fashioned 'stand and deliver' style.

The other problem is that the Arena doesn't have all the technical advantages of a modern theatre, so scene changes take a long time. A show that started at 9.15 didn't end until 1.00 in the morning. And in these seats (and these weren't the cheapest), that's a lot of time. We'd read about the famously uncomfortable seating, but nothing can prepare you for the reality. They are bum-achingly uncomfortable.

That apart it was an extremely enjoyable evening and the football added to the atmosphere. If you're a purist be warned that there will be regular flashing from cameras and – during the big numbers – applause will start before the orchestra has finished playing. It's not a place to listen and watch in reverential silence. The shared experience is what's important. If you have an interest in opera, it's a place you need to go to, at least once.

But take a cushion.

The weather ultimately defeated me.

By the end of June, I had decided it was time to change from my all-black look. By the first week of July I conceded that it was finally too hot for a jacket. I didn't do this lightly. I don't like not wearing a jacket. Wearing one, I look like a man about town. Without one, I look like a man without a home, and I miss all those useful extra pockets. When I went into school in shirtsleeves, the rest of the class applauded.

This may give you an idea of how hot it had become.

An anti-cyclone somewhere off North Africa was fanning hot air in the direction of northern Italy. Everyone said it had been the hottest June in memory. Temperatures were around 30 °C during the day, but it felt much hotter. It was impossible to keep cool, or even to keep dry. Humidity was at 90 per cent and I wondered if we would drown if it reached 100.

In the space of two months I had made the journey from hat and coat, to jacket, to shirtsleeves and (God help me) even the occasional outbreak of shorts and sandals. There was only one place left to go, namely sitting around the house in my pants, and nobody wanted that.

The Italian meteorological office gave these anti-cyclones wonderful classical names. We sweltered our way through

Scipio, Charon, Ulysses, Minos, Nero and Caligula, only to find that the none-more-ominously entitled Lucifero was soon to blow into town. The Met Office was playing a dangerous game as there was nowhere to go after that; it ran the risk that if an even hotter one arrived it would be forced to call it Keith or Nigel.

There was an irony in having gone to great pains to rent a flat with a balcony only to find it too hot to sit outside. It was not a problem we ever encountered in Leith. I was proud of my self-restraint in never using the words 'Remember that flat I liked that had air conditioning?'

It was a relief to get out of the city and on to the mainland where the humidity seemed a little more bearable.

A trip with the Istituto took us to Castelfranco, an historic walled town twenty-five miles from Venice. It's worth a visit in its own right but the main attraction is the cathedral, which houses the *Castelfranco Madonna*, one of a handful of undisputed paintings by Giorgione, the most mysterious artist of the Italian Renaissance.

We know very little about him. In his ground-breaking work *The Lives of the Artists*, the sixteenth-century painter and writer Giorgio Vasari devoted only a few pages to him. He had probably been a student of Giovanni Bellini, but opinion is divided as to whether he was Titian's master or if they were colleagues.

Giorgione seems to have been a handsome if foppish-looking fellow, judging by his statue (a recent one but based on what may be a self-portrait) and died a suitably romantic death at an early age. Vasari claims that the artist, always something of a ladies' man, went to visit his lover without realising she was carrying the plague, with unfortunate, if predictable, consequences.

There is no firm agreement on the number of works in existence that can be definitively attributed to him. It may be as few as six. Three of these are in Venice: a sad fragment of fresco from the outside of the Fondaco dei Tedeschi, and two works in the Accademia – *La Vecchia* and the mysterious *La Tempesta*. Mysterious in that nobody knows what it represents – it's not based on religious or classical themes, if it's an allegory it's impenetrable, and the one thing we know with certainty is that it isn't called *La Tempesta*. Giorgione. He's very mysterious.

The *Castelfranco Madonna* was commissioned by the mercenary Tuzio Constanzo in honour of his son Matteo, who had died of a fever during military service. It's a variation on the standard *sacra conversazione* and the composition is the classic triangle-within-rectangle style, but with a number of intriguing differences. It's assumed the figure on the right is St Francis, but the armoured figure on the left is more difficult to identify – he may be Saint George, local boy St Liberalis, or Matteo Constanzo himself. The coat of arms beneath the Virgin's throne is that of the Constanzo family, and the tomb and paved floor reflect the space of the chapel in which the painting is housed.

The background is most likely that of Castelfranco *c*.1505, and the importance given to the landscape is another thing that marks this work out as unusual – it wasn't common in Venetian painting of the time and Giorgione's use of it may have influenced his master Bellini. Great as he was, Bellini wouldn't have been able to resist adding a cloud of *putti* and an extraneous angel or two. Giorgione, however, keeps the composition clean and uncluttered, save for two tiny figures in the background. This painting isn't meant to inspire us to great, devotional thoughts – it's inviting us to pay our respects to the young Matteo.

Whatever it 'means', it's a magnificent work. There were five of us in our group, and we stood and looked at it and discussed it for almost thirty minutes. When you see the *Mona Lisa*, or the *Primavera*, or *The Birth of Venus*, you share the experience with hundreds of other people and the incessant click and flash of cameras. In this quiet chapel, in a town one hour from Venice, you can have one of the great paintings of the world to yourself.

Escaping to the Lido offered further respite from the heat. The district of Malamocco is one of the oldest parts of Venice, dating back to the sixth century when it was established by refugees from Padua.

Sometime during the twelfth century, a fisherman on the lookout for firewood spotted a hefty log and took it back to his house. The following morning, he discovered that it was no longer there. Off he went and, to his surprise, found it in the same place from which he'd taken it the previous day. Strange, but it was evidently a good log because he dragged it home once more.

The following morning, again, it was nowhere to be found. He went out and brought it home for a third time, with predictable results. You might think this was God's way of saying *go and pick a different log*, but our boy was not to be deterred, went back to the same place and, for his pains, was rewarded with a vision of the Virgin. He used the log to carve a statue of the Madonna and Child which, to this day, stands in the church of Santa Maria Assunta. Every year, a *sagra* is held to celebrate the event.

Our guide was Riccardo, a resident of the Lido and a lovely, hippyish chap. By day, he teaches Italian to immigrant schoolchildren. By night he plays bass in fearsome-sounding Venetian heavy metal band HausMaster, although he bemoans that, unlike Germany or the UK, Italy does not have a 'metal' culture. He believes that English is 'the language of metal' and that he learned more from the lyrics of Iron Maiden than he ever did at school. He admits that his English would be limited once conversation progressed beyond the themes of Death, Destruction and the Great Beast.

The *sagra* is small, but there's a good atmosphere to Malamocco. It's little more than a couple of streets, but it has something of the feel of a mini-Venice in the countryside and a genuine sense of community.

We took a look around the church (the priest was delighted to have visitors and showed us round everything, prior to insisting that we take some fruit from the garden) and visited a couple of art exhibitions. An archery demonstration caught my eye because, instead of the usual bull's eye target, they were using the image of the Welsh flag. It's possible that the great Wales–Venice conflict was one of the more unusual episodes in European history, and I should have been paying more attention in school that day; but I suppose it's more likely they thought it a striking image to engage the kids. The elderly gentleman in charge asked me if I could write something in the visitors' book, in Welsh. It's been thirty years since I used it in anger, but I can still remember the odd bit, and I thought the chance of a native speaker wandering along and shaking his head at the lamentable standards of Welsh language teaching in Malamocco was pretty remote. I limited myself to writing '*Pob Hwyl*' (All the best) and a translation ('*significa "Salutare"*'). He seemed disappointed at my indecipherable scrawl and added the words '*in lingua gallese*' next to it, in case anyone should be in doubt.

A band was setting up for later on and a number of stalls were selling local produce, but we feared a losing battle with the mosquitoes and made our way back to the vaporetto.

There may not be a huge amount to see, but it's a nice place and a refreshing change of pace from the hustle and bustle of the main islands. If you're in Venice for a long period, it repays a visit.

Three months of intensive study came to an end with a brutal two hours on pronominal verbs and a more enjoyable discussion of Dante. I have read all of the *Divina Commedia*. Not just the famous bits, or the gorier parts of the Inferno, but the whole lot, albeit in English. I felt smug for approximately ten seconds, when one of the other students said she had read it in its entirety in Italian. This was both deflating and confusing at the same time. If you can read the *Commedia* in the original language, you should probably be teaching Italian instead of studying it.

I had mixed feelings about finishing the course. I had enjoyed almost every minute of it, even the pronominals and the pleonastic *nons*. Studying had given a structure to our days, as well as a ready-made social calendar and supply of friends. I had the nagging thought that one month more and I would truly, properly master this language.

And yet there had been the occasional moment of thinking that old ground was being covered. Perhaps it was now more important to step back, to take stock of everything we'd covered and get out and speak Italian.

Caroline had enjoyed it somewhat less, perhaps because our minds work in different ways. She used to be a systems analyst – in other words she likes to revise and review everything until it's absolutely perfect. I was a programmer – I get on with things and, if it isn't 100 per cent correct, I can usually put it right without too much harm being done. This is a useful attitude for learning a language (it is also a terrible attitude for pursuing a career in IT).

The Istituto claimed to have dragged us up to level C1 ('Effective Operational Proficiency') of the Common European Language Framework, which is nearly as good as it gets. Even now, this is flattering us. Still, if there was no danger of us being mistaken for locals, we could now do everything we needed to, and it was something to build on. If you want to improve your Italian at the same time as taking a break in Venice, I highly recommend it.

Chapter 9

We were now left to our own devices for the first time since we arrived. There was no more red tape to deal with and we were no longer starting the day with four hours of Italian. Everything seemed that bit more normal – get up, go to the shops, get the paper; and then home for two hours of Italian revision and two hours of job hunting. We didn't have the Istituto to organise our social lives for us any more, but we still managed to entertain ourselves. The great Venetian *Festa del Redentore* was upon us. And here, a brief history lesson might be of use . . .

Titian's *Pietà* is my favourite painting in the Accademia. Dating from 1575, it's regarded as being his final work and the kneeling figure of Nicodemus before the body of Christ is likely a self-portrait. The impression is one of despair, of a flickering source of light being crushed under the weight of the encroaching darkness. There is little hope in this painting, and with good reason: Venice was in the grip of a plague that would kill a third of the population. Titian, a devout man, painted this as an act of supplication, a plea for himself and his son Orazio to be spared. It didn't work. The plague took them both, along with nearly fifty thousand others. The citizens of Venice believed it to be a punishment from God. It must have seemed like the end of the world.

The disease burned itself out in its own good time. In July 1576 the city was declared plague-free and, in 1577, ground was broken on Andrea Palladio's church of Il Redentore ('The Redeemer'), commissioned in thanks for the city's deliverance. To this day, the city celebrates the *Festa del Redentore* on the third Sunday in July.

Our *Redentore* started on the Thursday night, with a performance of *La Maschera della Morte Rossa* – The Masque of the Red Death. Devoid of dialogue and barely a few pages in length, Edgar Allan Poe's story is difficult to stage. This was a clever adaptation, however, and it worked well – a narrator related the story, which was acted out with a mixture of dance, music and *commedia dell'arte*, while the mirrored hall of the Palazzo Zenobio was the perfect space for it. Do be warned, however, never to sit in the front row of any performance in which the words *commedia dell'arte* are mentioned – your participation will be expected, nay, insisted upon . . .

We caught a boat to Giudecca on the Friday night and made our way to Il Redentore for a concert of early Italian baroque music. Palladio's church is notable for its cleanness of line and simplicity. There are no great baroque tombs or spiralling columns here. The impression is of space and light. Some might think it cold and clinical (Palladio's classicism sent the great John Ruskin into a fury), but it could be considered a perfect response to the circumstances that led to its commissioning. The concert – Monteverdi, Frescobaldi, Schuetz *et al.* – was first class; excellent playing and singing from the small group of musicians, filling the space wonderfully.

Saturday is the eve of the *Festa*. In the past, a bridge of boats would be constructed across the Giudecca canal. That stopped some years ago and today a temporary pontoon is used instead. At 7 p.m., Capuchin monks from the Redentore set out across the bridge to greet the Mayor and the Patriarch, who made their way back to the church to light candles in thanks, shortly followed by what seemed like the entire population of Venice.

The festival has a reputation as the most 'local' of Venice's celebrations and foreign accents were drowned out by Italian ones. The Zattere and the Giudecca were lined with people, many of whom were setting out chairs and tables, food and drink, in preparation for a long night. Others arrived in their boats and dropped anchor in the *bacino* – fewer than usual, however, due to the recent introduction of controversial new licensing measures.

We considered crossing the bridge, but the weight of the crowd put us off and we retired to Nico's for Negronis. An indulgence but the Redentore comes but once a year. Then home for dinner, following which we took a bottle of wine and some deckchairs to the *altana* to watch the fireworks. I thought we might have been spoilt by years of the Edinburgh fireworks at the festival and Hogmanay, but there was something incredibly special about seeing the city lit up like this.

Sunday felt clearer and cooler after an almighty storm, which sadly brought down all the lanterns lining the Zattere. There was a steady stream of traffic on the bridge, but we took our stroll over the canal to the church. It was an odd

feeling, despite the fact we'd made the same journey by vaporetto any number of times. Masses were being held round the
clock at the Redentore, with candles being consumed at such
a rate that a server was having to use a fish slice to clear away
excess wax.

We made our way across the only-slightly-ominously
wobbly bridge. A regatta of small boats was taking place in
the canal and, if you screwed your eyes up and tried to ignore
Porto Marghera and the floating gin palaces, you could
convince yourself that things hadn't changed much at all.

Venice, as I have said, is a great source of free music. But
there is also the opera house of La Fenice. Tickets, unfortunately, are not cheap, but we treated ourselves to a one-off
'Opera Gala' in the courtyard of the Ducal Palace, conducted
by the great Korean Myung-whun Chung, featuring an all
Verdi/Puccini programme for a modest thirty euros each.

We picked up our tickets and, finding ourselves with some
time on our hands, thought we could sneak in a swift one.
The area around Piazza San Marco is not the place to find
oneself in need of a quiet drink, but we found somewhere a
couple of streets away. It was a strange little place with an
interior festooned with girly calendars. I'm not quite sure
what their target market is, but perhaps it isn't the middle-
aged classical music fan.

We stood outside with our drinks, and I was pondering
that, presumably, it was somebody's job to turn all those
calendars over on the first of every month, when Caroline dug
me in the ribs. I was about to protest that I hadn't even raised
my eyes from my prosecco when she pointed to a gentleman

of South-East Asian appearance strolling past. *That's him, isn't it? That's the conductor.*

I wasn't convinced, as I'd seen Myung-whun before and I thought he was older and greyer. I said he was probably a tourist, albeit armed with something that looked like a music folder.

But, thirty minutes later, in the splendid surroundings of the Ducal Palace, it turned out that I was wrong, as the same gentleman walked to the podium. It had been Mr Chung. My apologies, *maestro*, you are clearly much younger than I thought.

This brought to mind an incident of a few days before, when I had almost bumped into the Patriarch of Venice. Literally. I turned my head and there he was, hurrying past in his work clothes. The city is a great leveller. The nature of the place makes it unlikely that you can be chauffeured from post to post and so the great and the good have to get around town in the same way as the rest of us, whether they be a famous international conductor, God's Representative in Venice, or a pair of unemployed ex-IT workers.

It was a splendid concert. With a decent orchestra, singers and conductor you can't go wrong with a programme of the best bits from *Butterfly*, *Tosca*, *Bohème*, *Don Carlo*, *Traviata et al.*; and the setting made it more special. We got an encore of the *William Tell* overture (Chung's an enjoyably 'visual' conductor when he has something like this to get his teeth into) and the 'Brindisi' from *La Trav*, which sent everyone home in a good mood.

We set off back to Santo Stefano, passing some musicians from the orchestra as we walked. They were making their way home through the *calli* like the rest of us.

*　　*　　*

Stravinsky in the twentieth century. Wagner in the nine-teenth. Mozart in the eighteenth. Monteverdi in the seven-teenth. *La Serenissima* has been a magnet for great compos-ers from the time of the Flemish musicians who came in the fifteenth and sixteenth centuries. Most significant of those, perhaps, was the figure of Adrian Willaert, who became the *Maestro di Cappella* at San Marco in 1527. Remaining until his death in 1562, he transformed the city's reputation from a musical backwater into one of the greatest in Europe. Composers came from all over the continent to study with him. Among his pupils was the great Venetian Andrea Gabrieli – an indelible link between the 'Venetian School' and the music of the Low Countries. It was a pleasure to attend a concert of polyphonic Flemish music at San Moisè one Saturday night.

San Moisè is a strange church. As you enter, the eye is drawn to the huge altarpiece, by Heinrich Meyring, of Moses receiving the Ten Commandments on Mount Sinai. Or, to be more precise, an almost actual-size reproduction of Mount Sinai. You have to admire the sheer bonkers ambition of it, even if the overall effect raises a smile instead of a sense of awe, which presumably wasn't Meyring's intention.

The programme was a selection from some of the greatest composers of that period – Ockeghem, Dufay, des Prez and Willaert himself. This is diabolically difficult music to sing and – with just four singers – there was no way that mistakes could be hidden. But if there was the occasional problem of intonation, it didn't detract from the excellence of the performance. It was fantastic music-making and that a concert of this quality was free was extraordinary.

Adrian Willaert is an unsung hero these days. By contrast, you couldn't get away from Vivaldi if you wanted to. You can see a concert of his works at San Vidal or the Pietà almost every night of the week. These are professional musicians, so it's fair to expect a certain standard of performance, but the problem is if you had to plough your way through *The Four Seasons* night after night after night, you would be forgiven for becoming a little stale. Do yourself a favour and seek out some of the free music in Venice. And save a few euros into the bargain.

I was getting used to our tiny kitchen by now, although the heat made it uncomfortable to spend any prolonged amount of time in there. Cooking had to be limited to dishes that could be put together relatively quickly. Great steaming risottos, requiring continuous stirring, were out. Quick pasta dishes were in.

Some years ago, in Sicily, we'd come across *bottarga*: dried tuna or grey mullet roe, cured in sea salt. It doesn't sound like the most appetising dish in the world and our initial impression was that it was nothing more than OK.

One of the fishmongers in Campo Santa Margherita told us he'd acquired some tuna with their roe and was having a go at making his own. He seemed pleased that we showed an interest. So much so that, one Saturday, Caroline arrived home from shopping with a great slab that he'd given her for free; and nothing says 'welcome to Venice' quite like free fish from the market.

Despite having been underwhelmed the previous time, I set to work on finding some recipes. There aren't many and they don't stretch much further than these :

Bruschetta with Bottarga
Ingredients: bread, bottarga
Method: grate bottarga over bread
Pasta with Bottarga
Ingredients: pasta, bottarga
Method: grate bottarga over pasta

Spaghetti with bottarga it was, then. There are any number of recipes, but I went with the *River Café* cookbook. I don't know why, but I've got it into my head that *The Silver Spoon* – the alpha and omega of Italian cooking – is for a regular dinner, but *River Café* gets pressed into service for something more special.

Except that this recipe seemed odd. I was scaling down the quantities but that only required the ability to divide by three and I was sure I'd got it right. It seemed to require 80 g of spaghetti to 100 g of bottarga, which was most of the chunk. It seemed like a hell of a lot. I cut a small piece off and nibbled away pensively. Quite nice, but it packed a hefty anchovy-like flavour and that much was going to make the dish a little assertive to say the least. I was prepared to give it a go, however, and got ready to start grating.

Caroline was less convinced and checked out recipes on the internet. There seemed to be no common agreement on quantities beyond the basic one of 'more bottarga than spaghetti is insane'.

In the event, I used a third of the amount and it was absolutely delicious.

Here is the adapted recipe.

Bottarga Jonesy

Ingredients (for 2): 175 g spaghetti, 60 g grated bottarga, as much garlic and parsley as you can be bothered to chop finely, half a deseeded dried chilli (I'd use a whole one. Caroline wouldn't use one at all. We compromised.)

Method: while the spaghetti is cooking, gently fry the garlic in a healthy slug of olive oil. Throw in the parsley and half the bottarga. Throw in the drained spaghetti, give it all a good stir and sprinkle the rest of the bottarga on top. Eat, with copious quantities of wine. Any colour will do.

A twenty-minute dinner and, thanks to our friendly fishmonger, practically free. If you're using *River Café*, don't forget to double-check those quantities.

The bottarga, having proved a success, prompted us to expand our horizons further.

Nervetti – we'd seen these listed occasionally in butcher's shops. We didn't know what they were and it proved difficult to find out. The dictionary translation defines them as 'nerves'. What do nerves taste like? For that matter, what do they look like? They didn't sound like something that needed to be tried in a hurry.

Caroline discovered *insalata di nervetti* on sale at the deli counter in Billa and decided we could afford to try 100 g of them, just in case. A search on the net showed me that they aren't nerves at all, but a tastier-sounding blend of pressed tendons and meat from a calf's hoof.

Sunday lunchtime arrived, and out they came.

We looked at them. A pile of semi-translucent, greyish, jelly-like cubes.

All of a sudden, 100 g seemed a bit of a challenge.

It would have been silly to come this far and not give them a go, so we tucked in. I say 'tucked in', but really mean that we half-heartedly prodded around looking for the more appetising bits. I found a small scrap that was a bit greyer than the others and took this as a sign that it was one of the meatier pieces.

You couldn't say they were horrible. You couldn't even say they were particularly unpleasant. They had a mild flavour of onions (unsurprising as they came packaged with a garnish of, well, onions) and not much else. If cold, slightly oniony jellyish cubes are your thing, you might find them a bit of a treat.

Cucina povera – the art of making tasty, nutritious food from the simplest and cheapest of ingredients – is one of Italy's great gifts to the world. The insistence on using every bit of the animal is commendable. I have winkled a tiny rabbit brain from its skull in a restaurant on Ischia. I have enjoyed crispy sheep brains in the Roman ghetto. I have eaten spleen-in-a-bun in a market in Palermo. *Nervetti*, however, were just a little too *povera*. Neither of us thought we needed to try them again.

Barrow upon Soar is not a large village but I managed to get myself lost. Caroline needed some products from Boots and, with the weather playing up, the walk into town was going to make a mess of her hair. I took the easy Bonus Hubby Points on offer and volunteered to go myself. My new brother-in-law had given me directions: take the first turning right, then the footpath past the school and you'll come to the main street.

I found myself in the middle of a housing estate, in a light linen suit perfect for a Venetian summer and less so for a wet and windy day in the English Midlands. I took a left and walked along the road for five minutes. Houses. I turned round and tried another way. More houses. I gave up and started again. I had somehow chosen the least obvious of the three paths I could have taken. I tried once more and, blessedly, shops appeared. After five minutes shopping I headed back to the house as if setting out for a jaunty stroll along the Zattere, past the bemused gaze of the locals kitted out with weatherproof coats and umbrellas, bracing themselves against the icy rain.

The rain. Proper, cold rain dropping from a slate-grey English sky. I felt ridiculously happy. It was tempting to stretch out on the grass and lie there, being rained on, but it struck me that passers-by might be concerned.

We had returned to the UK for a couple of days to celebrate my sister's wedding and I should have paid more attention to the weather forecast, because we now had thirty minutes before being pitched into the round of buttonholes, photos and welcome drinks. I looked like I'd been dragged backwards through a soggy hedge. I did not look like somebody who ought to be in a wedding photograph.

Caroline worked on my suit with a hairdryer. This used up the Bonus Hubby Points, but at least I was looking vaguely presentable by the time our lift arrived.

It was a warm, cheery and just-boozy-enough affair. Everybody had a good time, and my dad made the speech of his life. Helen looked frail, but happy.

Twenty-four hours later we were home. It seemed strange to be thinking of Venice as home, but that's what it was now. It was late evening when we arrived at Marco Polo, the night air taking the edge off the heat. The *capitano* on the Alilaguna boat into town was a cheerful fellow, listening to opera as he drove us through an almost-deserted Grand Canal. I thought what a nice job that must be at times. Two tourists were excitedly leaning out of the windows as far as they could, taking photographs and exclaiming at everything.

I envied them. They were seeing it all for the first time.

In the event of having to ask for directions in Venice you will likely be given the answer *sempre dritto*. This literally translates as 'straight ahead' but means 'head in that sort of direction for the next three *campi*, then turn left and cross the first bridge, then take the *calle* on the left or right – doesn't matter which, they both end up in the same place – and you should be in Campo San Luca, because every walk through San Marco seems to take you through Campo San Luca at some point. And then I think you'll need to ask someone else.'

It's not an attempt to fob off the tourist, but navigating is so damn complex you'd forget any proper directions soon enough anyway. And Venice's peculiar geography means that *sempre dritto* will get you to where you want to go. Eventually.

I returned home late from the cinema one evening. Late enough for the men selling bags and the tat merchants to have called it a night, so I was surprised when I turned into Campo Santo Stefano and someone called out 'Excuse me sir . . .?'

It was a couple in need of directions. They wanted to get to San Marco, but were walking towards the Accademia Bridge.

I began explaining that they were already in the right district, but for the Piazza itself they needed to head in the opposite direction.

The young woman complimented me on my English, but her bloke recognised my accent and grinned. 'South Wales, right?' It turned out he was from Wrexham. This would normally be an occasion for manly hugs and perhaps even a spritz, but it was pushing midnight and I wanted to get home. Sadly, The Only Other Welshman in Venice was also The Unluckiest Welshman in Venice as, of all the people he could have asked for directions, he had asked the man who got lost in Barrow upon Soar.

I took a look at their map, and pointed out Campo Santo Stefano and Piazza San Marco. I have my own method of getting there, but it's called 'following Caroline' and I wasn't sure I could prod her out of bed at five to midnight and ask her to escort two strangers on their way. I pointed in the general direction and smiled. 'It's *sempre dritto*,' I said.

I hope they made it.

Chapter 10

Venice, and indeed much of Italy, closes down in August. This does not mean that the city appears any less crowded, but anyone who is able heads out of the city to the mountains or to the seaside. Bars, restaurants, shops and newspaper kiosks are shut down, with 'closed for the holidays' signs hanging outside.

Work, we knew, was something that we would soon have to tackle. In the meantime, there were places to explore and *sagre* or *feste* to attend. There was no shortage of them. Whether it be for saints, vegetables, shellfish or revolutionary communism, the Venetians can turn anything into a celebration.

Ferragosto was originally a celebration of the middle of summer and the end of hard manual work in the fields, but it also serves as a religious holiday for the Assumption of the Virgin.

Given the number of churches dedicated to the Blessed Virgin Mary, you'd think this would be the cue for celebrations throughout the city. They're mainly confined, however, to the remote island of Torcello and its basilica.

Torcello was one of the first islands in the lagoon to be settled. Until the eleventh century it was more powerful than Venice itself, but the island fell into decline as problems with malaria intensified. It lies in the area known, ominously, as the Dead Lagoon.

It seems hard to imagine now, but twenty thousand people once lived on Torcello. Today, there are just eleven. That's eleven, not eleven thousand. The journey there takes approximately an hour and, once you arrive, a ten-minute walk will lead you to what passes for the centre of town; the majority of the mediaeval structures having been scavenged for building materials over the centuries.

What remains is the church of Santa Fosca, the Palazzo dell'Archivio and the Palazzo del Consiglio, which together make up the provincial museum; and, most importantly, the Basilica of Santa Maria Assunta. A church has stood on this site since the seventh century and was remodelled into its current form around the year 1000 – remodelled in a bit of a hurry as there was a belief that the world was going to end by the turn of the millennium and they wanted to have it ready in time.

Where do you start with this building? You could look down, to the mosaic floor; or up, to the intricately sculpted white marble capitals that impressed the never-knowingly-overwhelmed John Ruskin. But, likely as not, your eye will be drawn to the extraordinary mosaic on the west wall. The Last Judgement. *Giudizio Universale.* Or, should you be feeling apocalyptic, the Doomsday Mosaic. Christ sits in judgement as the souls of the departed are weighed; while those who don't make the cut are prodded downwards into a river of fire by a group of sorrowful-looking angels, where the Antichrist, sitting on Satan's knee, insouciantly ushers them into Hell, the trace of a smile upon his lips.

It's enormous fun (although that presumably wasn't the intention) but the greatest work of art on Torcello, and one of the greatest in all of Venice, is directly opposite. It's an attenuated mosaic image of the Virgin, alone in the golden space of the apse. This is the Virgin *Theotokos*, the 'God-bearer', a tall, thin young woman holding the Christ child. Whereas the Doomsday Mosaic is all action, this is quiet and powerful in its simplicity. She gazes at us as if barely controlling an unbearable pain; as if she were holding each one of us responsible for what is to come.

By contrast, there isn't much art in the church of Santa Fosca, but it's a calm, cool, reflective space; and, for those with a particular interest in bits of saints, the remains of Santa Fosca and Santa Maura are held in an illuminated case under the altar. We spent about thirty minutes in the archaeological museums and then it was enough of the high culture and time for lunch.

The Osteria al Ponte del Diavolo (named for the nearby and less-exciting-than-you-might-think Devil's Bridge) is one of our favourite restaurants in Venice. Caroline had an elegant dish of dressed crab, before moving on to pasta with lobster. I started with a dish of pasta with black truffle, followed by the greatest plate of fried fish in the world, a big crispy pile of vegetable strips, squid, prawns and miscellaneous (and unidentifiable) 'little fish'.

We should have left it there. At the least we should have gone for a post-lunch snooze on the comfy-looking loungers in the garden. But there was a concert in the Basilica, so we made our way back. Lunch had been a bit too leisurely, however, and we were unable to find a seat with a view. Vivaldi and Boccherini: pleasant enough, but neither of us were in the mood to appreciate it. As one quickly learns in Venice, there'll always be more Vivaldi.

I prefer not to dwell on the journey back. Everyone on the island, including the orchestra, seemed to be getting the same boat. Crammed into the vaporetto, in steaming thirty-something heat, it resembled a floating Black Hole of Calcutta. But all in all, it had been a very good day.

Neither of us needed our tea.

> *... as in the Arsenal of the Venetians*
> *boils in winter the tenacious pitch*
> *to smear their unsound vessels over again*
> *for sail they cannot; and instead thereof*
> *one makes his vessel new, and one recaulks*
> *the ribs of that which many a voyage has made;*
> *One hammers at the prow, one at the stern;*
> *This one makes oars and that one cordage twists;*
> *Another mends the mainsail and the mizzen.*
>
> Dante, 'Inferno', *Divine Comedy*,
> Canto XXI, verses 7–15

Dante's words are chiselled into the walls of the Arsenale, behind a pride of lions sculpted by someone who might have heard of such an animal but had only a vague notion of what one looked like.

Dating to the thirteenth century, the Arsenale anticipated the mass production of the industrial revolution by almost six hundred years. At its peak, this great engine of commerce and war employed 16,000 workers, capable of producing a ship a day. Napoleon destroyed various parts and added others, without knowing what to do with it, before passing it on to the Austrians who didn't have much idea either. Today, large parts of it serve as exhibition space during the Venice Biennale, but it still functions as a naval base.

A recent initiative had allowed visitors in to see some of the previously inaccessible military areas, as part of a guided tour *al chiaro di luna* – by the light of the moon.

There was already a crowd by the time we arrived and it transpired we had a problem: a German family were the only ones who didn't speak Italian. It wasn't their fault, it hadn't been advertised as Italian-only, but our guide apologised and said that she didn't speak German. They asked if she could explain the main bits in English, but – more firmly this time – she declined. Things seemed to be getting off to a fractious start, until Caroline prodded me and suggested I could act as interpreter. The Germans smiled. The guide smiled. I smiled, weakly. Everyone seemed happy with this, so I agreed to give it a go.

As soon as the tour started, I realised this was not going to work. I can't take Italian in and convert it directly into German. I have to mentally translate it into English and then find the German, which is not as easy as it used to be. By the time I'd done that the conversation had moved on. After a few stumbling attempts in a not-entirely-successful Italian/German hybrid, it was easier to translate into English, letting the anglophone members of the party pass it on to the others.

It's surprising how atmospheric and beautiful a military base can be by the light of the moon. The trouble is, the moonlight wasn't bright enough to see everything clearly. It was fascinating but, unfortunately, we couldn't see much of it. The tour had been overbooked and, at times, we had to walk in single file along unpaved tracks. I would translate as best I could for my German friends, make my way up the line to hear the next bit from the guide and then scurry back to pass it on, which meant we received a fragmentary description of the place.

It was an enjoyable evening, if harder work than I'd imagined. I wondered if some sort of tip might be forthcoming, but I was happy to settle for their good wishes. An interesting tour, if perhaps better suited to the daylight hours.

Another day and another *festa*, this time for San Rocco, whose *chiesa* is another of Venice's Plague Churches. It is an interesting building, although perhaps in need of some TLC; and inevitably overshadowed by the adjacent Scuola Grande.

The inside of the Scuola is covered in paintings by Jacopo Tintoretto (with help from his workshop and his son Domenico) who won a competition, in 1564, to decorate the Sala dell'Albergo. He didn't so much win as cheat: the Confraternity had only wanted initial sketches but Tintoretto found out the exact dimensions required for the ceiling painting, ran up a quick San Rocco in Glory and installed it in place. Cue much sucking of teeth and shaking of heads from the judges. This wasn't the done thing. Tintoretto shrugged and told them that if it was going to be a deal-breaker, he might be prepared to let them have it for free.

Swift mental calculations and more shaking of heads followed. OK, said Tintoretto, I'm cutting my own throat here, but as I've done the centrepiece now, what if I finished off the rest of it – add in a few allegories, that sort of thing – and let you have the whole ceiling free, gratis and for nothing?

This was highly irregular, but nonetheless ... the whole ceiling? That sounded like a good deal.

Tintoretto, having 'won' the competition, set to work on the mighty Crucifixion that covers one wall of the Sala, and moved on to an *Ecce Homo*, Christ before Pilate and a Road to Calvary on the opposite wall.

There was no stopping him. The ceiling of the Sala Superiore depicts most of the Book of Exodus and the walls relate the life of Christ. Downstairs, in the Sala Terrena, he rattled through the life of the Virgin from Annunciation to Assumption. Some of these may not be among his best works in Venice (Ruskin was lukewarm on a number of them, and particularly disappointed by the frumpy Virgin of the Annunciation) but the overall effect is overwhelming. If Venice has an equivalent of the Sistine or Scrovegni chapels, it's here.

Entrance was free for the *festa*, together with one of those serious in-depth Italian tours. Our guide, a *Confratello*, showed us round every work, a process that took over two hours. He explained their theological and historical significance in relation to the philosophy of the Confraternity. He digressed in order to discuss their relevance in the context of the Council of Trent (of which, he evidently assumed, we had an in-depth knowledge). And yet, it was all so fascinating we forgot to feel tired and even stopped fretting about the heat.

After covering the upper floor, we were shown a couple of works on easel, one by Titian, another by the school of Giorgione. They might have been the standout works in any other space but, in the midst of all this splendour, we gave them a cursory glance and a shrug of 'Yeah. Titian.'

Finally, we were finished. We lost a few along the way but nearly all of the group had stuck it out to the end. The guide smiled and said he'd see us next year. As it turned out, I'd be back the next month.

'So what are the Communists up to tonight?' A question we frequently asked ourselves during the Festa di Liberazione in Campo San Giacomo dell'Orio, organised by the Partito della Rifondazione Comunista.

Every evening followed a similar pattern of a political discussion or presentation, followed by some music. A number of stalls sold beer, wine and snacks. Petitions were signed. T-shirts were sold with the word 'Peace' in a dozen different languages, including Welsh (*Heddwch*, if you're interested).

The first night concerned the plight of workers in a factory in Marghera, where the management were offshoring jobs despite the business turning in good profits. Most of the people around us seemed to be there for the beer and food, and kept talking throughout, which made it difficult to follow. The following night sounded more interesting, with a play entitled *L'eclisse della Democrazia*, centring on the anti-globalisation G8 demonstrations in Genova in 2001.

Leftie things usually start a bit late. Italian things usually start a bit late. With this in mind, there was no need for us to turn up fifteen minutes early to be sure of getting a good seat. With five minutes to go, the audience consisted of ourselves, a man with an iPad and two small boys on bikes, circling the seating area like Indians around a wagon train.

The seats filled up over the following forty-five minutes, but with no sign of it starting. The man with the iPad must have been wondering if the battery life really was the advertised ten hours; the small boys seemed willing to keep their circuit going all night.

An hour passed, but it was no real hardship. San Giacomo dell'Orio is one of the loveliest squares in Venice and it was a pleasure to sit around, with the occasional journey to the bar where drinks were being sold at comradely prices.

The show kicked off, a one-man piece interspersed with music from an accordionist and clarinettist, based around events that Amnesty International have described as 'the most serious violation of human rights in a Western democracy since the end of World War II'.

Two hundred thousand demonstrators arrived in Genova in 2001, nearly a hundred of whom were in temporary accommodation in the Diaz-Pertini school. Following the discovery of a brace of Molotov cocktails, Italian police stormed the building and turned it into a temporary, illegal, detention centre. Over the course of the night, the protesters were systematically abused and beaten. Sixty were left with serious injuries, three of them comatose. A British journalist was beaten to a bloody pulp. Female detainees were threatened with rape.

The charges against all the detainees at Diaz were dropped, a judge concluding that they had put up no resistance and statements had been falsified. The deputy police chief later admitted that the Molotovs had been planted by police to justify the raid. Twenty-five officers were convicted of grievous bodily harm and planting evidence. The drawn-out appeals process, together with the statute of limitations in Italian law, means that none of them will go to jail.

The events at Diaz still have resonance in Italy, because it serves as a reminder that when the wrong people have their hands on the levers of power it doesn't take much for a liberal Western democracy to behave in a manner that can only be described as fascist. And, for ourselves, still in the honeymoon period of our relationship with Italy, and Venice, it served as a reminder: this is not Disneyland.

The evening concluded with tango dancing in the *campo*. As soon as the applause had finished, chairs were cleared away and audience members changed into their dancing shoes. We have vague memories of learning a social foxtrot for our wedding, but decided that this was beyond us. We departed for the next vaporetto, leaving the comrades to tango the night away.

Caterina Cornaro is perhaps the most significant female figure in Venetian history. In 1468, at the age of fourteen, she was betrothed to James II of Cyprus, and married him four years later. James died in 1473, leaving his young wife to act as regent to their infant son. When the younger James died before his first birthday, Caterina was left to rule the kingdom alone, until 1489 when she abdicated in order that Venice might attain control of Cyprus. Her return to Venice is marked to this day by the *Corteo*

Storico, the historical parade that makes up part of the annual *Regata Storica*.

The *Corteo Storico* puts a cheerier spin on the historical reality: Caterina had not wanted to abdicate, but was forced to do so through a mixture of threats and bribery. Venice – through a cynical but clever and far-sighted piece of realpolitik – got what it wanted with control of a strategically important site.

Caterina died in 1510 and is buried in the Chiesa di San Salvador. On the Saturday preceding the *Regata*, as a curtain-raiser to the main event, it hosted a concert in her memory; comprising four variations on the text of the *Salve Regina*.

There's always a good musical programme at San Salvador. The trouble is, it's an incredibly uncomfortable place to listen to music. The pews hold your back at an awkward angle, almost throwing you forward, and – if you're above a certain height – you can either sit with your chin resting on your knees, or slouch semi-horizontally, dangling your feet under the pew in front. There are two excellent Titians (the Transfiguration and the Annunciation) and a fake Bellini to take your mind off things.

Sunday was the day of the *Regata*. We made a quick circuit of possible viewing points along the Grand Canal, but nothing seemed satisfactory. In the end we took some deckchairs to Campo San Samuele, along with reading material and wine to while away the afternoon.

The *Corteo Storico* passed by, representing the entrance of Caterina and the Doge, followed by historic-looking barges, then locals in various degrees of period costume, rowing clubs and . . . anybody who had a boat who fancied joining in.

After the *Corteo*, the *Regata* proper began, consisting of races for different age groups and classes of boat. It was impressive, although of greater interest to those with a serious interest in rowing.

The event may play fast and loose with history, but that doesn't matter. It was a pleasant way to spend the afternoon, a layer of cloud keeping the sun off without threatening to rain.

Dinner that evening was a fine piece of tuna marinated in gin and red wine. An unusual combination of flavours, due to my mistake in assuming that *ginevra* translated as gin and not juniper. I think it worked.

Chapter 11

The seemingly endless procession of *feste* rolled on, whether they were religious, historical or political. There was no time to go to everything. The Film Festival finished without us ever really being aware that it had been on at all. There was coverage in the press every day, but unless you go out to the Lido, it's not inescapable in the same way as the Art Biennale.

It wasn't the only festival in town, as the great and the good of *la settima arte* found themselves competing for the public's affections with the Alberoni Festival of Mussels (or, in Veneziano, the *Festa del Peocio*).

It was a cheery if low-key affair – there is a limit to how much celebration you can build around a mollusc. There was a bouncy castle and football for the kids, and bands playing in the evening; but it was mainly an excuse to eat lots of mussels and none the worse for that.

More seriously, it's run in conjunction with the World Wildlife Fund to raise awareness of the complex ecosystem of the lagoon and the Alberoni dunes, specifically their efforts in sea turtle conservation. I had no idea there were sea turtles in that area of the Adriatic.

When we got home I took down a recently acquired cook-book that fell open at a recipe for turtle soup. This wasn't what I wanted to think about following an afternoon of reading about the exploits of cheery cartoon turtles. I stuffed a squid for dinner instead.

The year 2012 was the second annual *Isole in Rete* in which the public get the chance to visit some of the inaccessible islands of the north lagoon; while some of the others, on the regular transport network, host special events.

First on our itinerary was San Giacomo in Paludo (or St James-in-the-Marsh). This is a tiny spit of an island, not on any vaporetto route. It went through the usual cycle of many of the smaller, abandoned islands: monastery, dissolution, gunpowder store, and rack and ruin. Like many of them, it is now being looked after by the equivalent of the National Trust.

There isn't much to see now. Little remains of the monastery itself, the powder magazines are ruined; and many of the buildings are in a perilous condition due to the continual effect of *moto ondoso* (waves caused by continual motor traffic in the lagoon), and are therefore inaccessible. It's nice that people think enough of the place to give up their time and energy to look after it.

Mazzorbetto was next – technically an island in itself, although separated only by a few feet from the main body of Mazzorbo. The fort, an early twentieth-century structure, served as a Fascist holiday camp during the Mussolini era. It fell into ruin for fifty years, before being taken over by the Boy Scout movement. Annoyingly, we'd already gone for a mediocre lunch on Torcello, whereas we'd have been better off coming straight to Mazzorbetto and having the scouts grill us some sausages. A photographic exhibition recorded the history of the island during the twentieth century. There were images of hundreds of happy, smiling families from the 1920s, in what would be nothing more than nostalgic period photographs were it not for the presence of banners that chillingly read *Grazie, Duce.*

Mazzorbo was no more than ten feet away across a canal, but this was enough to compel us to wait for the next boat. It crossed my mind that, if I took a good run-up, I could leap to the other side. I got a mental image of the consequences of not making it and decided waiting was the better option. My long-jumping years are behind me if they were ever there at all.

Sant'Erasmo is on a standard route, but we stopped for an exhibition at the Torre Massimiliano, an imposing structure built when the Austrians were in charge.

It's used as an exhibition space these days, and was hosting a photographic display of fortified structures throughout Venice and the surrounding area. There were few captions, and it didn't take long before one photograph of a crumbling ruin started to resemble every other photograph of a crumbling ruin. We failed to find any sign of a supposed vineyard tour near the vaporetto stop and left thinking that it hadn't been worth the detour.

We had to get back to Venice, grab a bite to eat and catch a boat to Lazzaretto Nuovo for an evening concert by the Ensemble Vocale di Venezia. We had time for a spectacularly underwhelming pizza at a restaurant on the Fondamente

Nove, where even the waiter seemed embarrassed and looked at us as if to say, 'Yeah. I know.'

There was an almighty queue at the stop and not enough space for everyone on the boat. The organisers had anticipated this and laid on an extra service, which arrived ten minutes later. It was dark by the time we arrived, but the island was illuminated by a strip of citronella candles which served to light the path to the *lazzaretto*, the old quarantine station, and keep the clouds of mosquitoes at bay.

Crowds of people stood around, chatting and wondering what to do next, and then everyone began to fall silent. Something magical was happening. A boat emerged from the darkness and from across the water, barely perceptible at first, came the sound of a choir. They disembarked and – still singing – led us along the candlelit path and into the hall.

It was a wonderful concert of sacred and profane music, from Gabrieli and Palestrina up to the present day, taking in some enjoyably unexpected material along the way (John Dowland's 'Fine Knacks for Ladies' in Italian accents). I realised there were a number of familiar faces in the choir, singers I already knew from the Cantori Veneziani. Gianfranco, one of the basses, did a double-take when he spotted me in the crowd. We chatted for a while, and I asked him how he found time to be in two choirs. He shrugged, and said tonight's concert hadn't taken much rehearsing so it was no trouble to fit it in.

I found that remarkable given the quality of the singing. But there was more.

'You should sing with us, you know.'

'What, really?'

'Definitely. We could do with another bass. We start rehearsing again after the summer. Come along.'

And so I added another choir, and another group of friends, to my list.

We needn't have bothered with the disappointing pizza, as a buffet and drinks had been laid on for everyone afterwards. The evening ended on a downbeat note, however, when one grumpy-arsed member of the audience kicked up a fuss about having to pay for his ticket home. The organiser did his best to point out that – given that he had enjoyed a free concert and supper – paying for transport was not that iniquitous; but Mr Grumpy was having none of it and paid up with very bad grace. Personally, I'd have left him there to stew until the next boat arrived, which could have been anything up to a week, competing for the island's scant food resources with the suspiciously well-fed-looking cats . . .

The second day of *Isole in Rete* started with a visit to the Tenuta Scarpa Volo on Mazzorbo, an *agriturismo* project centring on the ideas of environmental education and organic agriculture. The holding includes a hostel, a smart-looking hotel and restaurant, and (this was the selling point for us) a vineyard. As part of the weekend's events, they'd arranged a series of one-hour guided tours.

It didn't work out that way. We turned up and stood by a pond for fifteen minutes while one of the guides explained the project to us. And that was it. It all seemed worthy and deserving of support, but I couldn't help thinking, *We got up early on Sunday morning to come out here and stand in a field and – crucially – we are not even going to try the wine!*

We were left to our own devices and we took a wander around the vineyard. It was pleasant but felt like a walk around a biscuit factory without being able to eat any biscuits.

We took a boat tour to the outer reaches of the lagoon in the afternoon. North-east of Torcello lies the island of Sant'Ariano. The bone island. The official cemetery of San Michele had limited space so, following ten years' interment, your remains would be exhumed and deposited on the ossuary island. If you were a normal inhabitant of Venice, this was where you ended up.

It isn't used any more and it's impossible to see what lies beyond the walls as it's completely overgrown. There's a tiny chapel (I could make out a crucifix but little else) and a jetty, with a warning sign advising that landing is strictly forbidden. The reasons are unclear, but I believe the stonework is crumbling and dangerous. I would love a closer look one day but it doesn't seem to be possible. Perhaps it's better left to the imagination.

We headed to the far reaches of the northern lagoon. Tiny scraps of land, long since pillaged for their stonework. On an island consisting of a ruined house, a battered sign read 'No Hunting'. The impression was of silence and desolation. I turned 180 degrees, towards the airport, and the illusion was shattered. But, for a moment, this had felt like the end of the line.

There were, we were forced to admit, just too many festivals. An alarming number were passing us by. *Venezia città viva* and the *Settimana culturale nell'isola per la citta* had come and gone, and even Extreme, the contemporary music biennale, had finished without us finding the time to see anything.

The Festival of Artichokes on Sant'Erasmo, earlier in the year, had proved an unexpected success, so we decided to go to the same island's *Festa del Mosto* (or the festival of wine must: the unfermented grape juice produced by the pressing – or treading – of grapes).

Sant'Erasmo gets busy on these occasions, so we were up early on Sunday morning to catch the boat from Fondamente Nove. The vaporetto was packed, but getting there thirty minutes in advance paid off and we got seats. So far, so good, until we reached the *Cappanone* stop (one before *Chiesa*, which is where the Festa was taking place) and the conductor announced to a disgruntled boatload of people that, in spite of what the timetable might have said, this was the end of the line. Everyone disembarked and began the long trek to the *chiesa*.

It was an oppressively hot day and we had no idea how long the walk was likely to be. After fifteen minutes we toyed with the idea of giving up and turning back, but we couldn't tell if we'd gone more than halfway. A young woman on a bicycle passed us in the opposite direction. A few minutes later she passed us again. I considered offering her money for her bike, but feared the gesture might be misinterpreted.

We walked for about thirty minutes until, rounding a corner, we saw the church ahead of us. A less welcome sight was that of a boat, in defiance of what we'd been told, steaming up to the jetty.

It had been a waste of time getting up early and we'd had an unnecessary walk as well, but hopefully the *Festa* would make up for it. It was OK-ish. Lunch was pleasant. There were a few stalls selling local produce. There were also some small children treading grapes (I think they were volunteers rather than their parents putting them to work in the fields) but grape-treading isn't a tremendously visual experience and after thirty seconds or so you've pretty much got the idea.

We took a look around the church (no great art, but interesting for its Fascist-period facade), bought a bottle of red wine *mosto* and decided to go home.

We stood in line at the *Chiesa* stop for ten minutes, caught the next vaporetto and settled into our seats. It had been a disappointing day but at least the boat wasn't too crowded.

Five minutes later the conductor announced that the service was terminating at *Cappanone*. We were disgorged onto the jetty into a seething crowd waiting for the next boat to Venice. We should all have moved to the back of the queue but nobody was going to do that in case they failed to get on, and the weight of numbers made it impossible. The result was a group, myself included, braced precariously on the edge of the jetty. If anyone behind tried to move forward, or even sneezed, I would end up in the lagoon.

The next boat arrived, but the captain didn't want to pull up to the mooring as he was afraid – with good reason – that somebody would get pushed in and be crushed between the jetty and the boat. He kept shouting for us to move back, but nobody wanted to lose their place and there was no way the crowd behind us were going to shift an inch. At one point it looked like he'd given up and was going to leave us there but, finally, he reversed in as slowly as he could. The conductor tried to get us to make way for the people getting off, but nobody could move. It took an age to get everybody out and the captain and conductor looked severely pissed off. It wasn't their fault but ACTV, the transport company, had fouled up badly by not taking account of the likely extra number of passengers.

We got back to the city and went for a consolatory beer at La Cantina. Inevitably, it was closed. It had all been hard work with nothing to show for it except 1.5 litres of red wine must. Which, splendidly, ended up saving the day. It was a pleasant sweet wine, perfect as an after-dinner drink, and it made a delicious red wine sauce for a roast duck. I'm not saying I'd rush back to the next agricultural festival on Sant'Erasmo but, just maybe, it had been worth the trouble after all.

During our first visit to the Venice Biennale, we had wandered around one of the off-site exhibitions and come across a room full of junk. Tools, bits of lumber, rubbish; that sort of thing. And, with our brains addled by two weeks of intensive contemporary art, we couldn't make up our minds if it was Art. Or a Shed. We decided it was a Shed (I'm still not 100 per cent sure that we were right) and, ever since, 'Art or Shed' has been our Occam's razor for those awkward 'Yes, but is it *art*?' questions.

The Architecture Biennale was by now in full swing, but we'd yet to pay much attention to it. Not through lack of interest, but there hadn't been enough time as other, more immediate, events kept getting in the way.

One of these was *LiberArti*, a free arts festival running over three days on Giudecca. It's very much a community affair. There were no grand parties for celebrities – the opening event was a ceremonial hanging of a home-made banner over the Ponte Lungo.

As you might expect from the name, everything was free. The bigger events were linked with the Biennale and not part of *LiberArti*, but together they made Giudecca one big, long art crawl. It took in almost every kind of space. Some were shops hosting a couple of pictures in the window. There were exhibitions in professional galleries, in *palazzi*, in a working men's club, in artists' studios, in the hall of somebody's house. There was also performance art, theatre and a screening of *Don't Look Now* – all of which we managed to miss, for reasons of geography and time.

Some of the art was just on an enthusiastic amateur level. But that wasn't important. What mattered was that it engaged people. People in galleries were eager to talk and there was a genuine sense of community about the event. We kept running into one of the organisers (Andrea, a lovely bloke from the excellent Bar Palanca) who was keen to recommend places to us.

As we crossed off exhibitions on the map, we encountered an abandoned headboard sporting a row of fairy lights. We stared for a while. There was supposed to be art in this spot, but could this be it? Was it Art? Or a Shed?

I'd been unable to make my mind up about Giudecca. It's a strange mixture of styles: typical Venetian buildings mix with modern blocks of flats and some shabbier parts. At the end of three days of *LiberArti* I decided I'd done it a disservice. It has its less attractive areas, but there's also a feeling of 'localness' here. It's Venice, but not quite as we know it, and much nicer than I'd thought.

The headquarters of the soon-to-be-defunct savings bank Cassa di Risparmio di Venezia in Campo Manin does not feature highly on any list of the city's most loved buildings.

It's a rare example of modernist architecture in the city and, the complaint goes, it doesn't fit the surrounding environment. I don't think it's a bad building – in other cities it might be thought of more highly – but it seems strange and out of place at first sight.

The history behind it is interesting. Towards the end of the nineteenth century, the city wanted a permanent monument to Daniele Manin, the hero of the rebellion against the Austrians. The church of San Paternian (already closed by Napoleon) was demolished to make way for the statue of Manin, and the square was renamed in his honour. In 1883, the first Cassa di Risparmio was opened. By the 1960s, the bank had outgrown the building, and a new one was commissioned which opened in 1972. It's worth stressing that the new building replaced one less than a century old – it's not as if an historic monument was demolished to make way for it.

The architects were Angelo Scattolin and the great Pier Luigi Nervi. We took a proper look around it during a one-day event called *Il Palazzo – Arte e Storia nelle banche* (think of it as a banks-only equivalent to Doors Open Day or Open House in the UK). We were taken round by one of the bank staff who explained its history. On the first day of business, he told us, the bank took the grand total of 1.5 lira in deposits; the one from a bishop and the half from an ordinary member of the public.

The interior feels spacious and full of light, due to a ceiling supported on just four pillars. I wasn't sure if I could take photographs – banks, understandably, get twitchy about that sort of thing – but the guide was happy for me to do so. Architecture students, he told me, are always particularly interested in the staircase, which shows the influence of Carlo Scarpa.

Beyond the architecture, there's some interesting art, and midway through the tour we were handed over to the bank's archivist. One of the board rooms holds a preparatory design for Tintoretto and his workshop's *Paradiso*, the full-scale version of which can be seen in the Palazzo Ducale. Another holds a portrait of a Venetian nobleman that is commonly attributed to Tintoretto's son Domenico. But, in the opinion of the archivist, it may be something more exciting: the lack of a signature and pentimenti (found throughout Domenico's work) might mean it is the work of Tintoretto's daughter Marietta, *la Tintoretta*.

He led us to the archive itself, where he put on a pair of white cotton gloves and reverently took down a small book, no more than five by three inches. *The Life of the Virgin*, he announced, and turned to the beautifully illustrated front page. It was painted by Bellini with a brush made, it is said, from the hair of a newborn baby . . .

The building is a controversial one. But in its unique way, it's one of the most interesting in the city.

The Fondazione Querini Stampalia hosted a number of events and exhibitions for the architecture biennale. Most of these were of modest interest; nevertheless, it's always a pleasure to visit. The attraction is the architecture of Carlo Scarpa; without doubt, the most important Venetian architect of the twentieth century. I'm embarrassed to admit that we weren't familiar with him before we became regular visitors to Venice, yet we'd encountered his work without being aware of it. If you've spent any time in Venice or Florence you've almost certainly seen examples of his architecture: he remodelled the space that holds the three great *Maeste* by Giotto, Cimabue and Duccio in the Uffizi; and renovated the picture galleries of both the Museo Correr and Accademia in Venice.

Spend some time with his work and you begin to understand why Luigi Nono lauded him as 'the architect of infinite possibilities'. His buildings are rarely flashy examples of 'superstar' architecture, but his work, and his influence, are to be found throughout the city. The Olivetti showroom that he designed as a calling card for the company is a hidden gem, lying almost unnoticed off Piazza San Marco. The ground floor of the Querini Stampalia was remodelled by him in the early 1950s and is, for my money, one of the most thrilling interiors in all Venice.

Head out to the *giardini* and you'll see his monument to the women partisans. Within the gardens are his ticket booth for the Biennale, the pavilion of Venezuela and the sculpture court of the central pavilion. Scarpa-influenced staircases and windows are a leitmotif in the city's modern, or remodelled, buildings.

If you only had a couple of days to spend, you could choose to ignore the traditional sites and build an itinerary solely around its modern architecture. That might seem wilfully perverse, but it would be a deeply cool thing to do.

Chapter 12

Caroline has always wondered why I don't sing more around the house. The answer is partly that I feel self-conscious, but it's mainly because repeating difficult sections over and over is going to become annoying, especially if it's a piece for which she doesn't care. I suppose it's unlikely that I'll ever be cast as Mozart's Queen of the Night but, if I were, I would have to check into a hotel for a couple of weeks. Even if there's a performance coming up I tend to concentrate on revising the score instead of singing out loud.

Which brings me back to Cantori Veneziani and my first concert with them – Leonard Bernstein's *Chichester Psalms* and Benedetto Marcello's setting of Psalm 36. Marcello is one of the most interesting figures in Venetian musical history. Composer, lawyer and politician, he served on Venice's Council of Forty, acted as governor of the city of Pola (now Pula in Croatia) and *camerlengo* – papal administrator – of Brescia; and still found time to compose hundreds of works. Among these is the *Estro poetico-armonico*, based on the text of the first fifty psalms and regarded as his greatest work.

Marcello, himself the subject of a long-forgotten opera by Joachim Raff, is an obscure figure in the UK. It's little wonder I'd never heard of him, as there's little of his music commercially available. And that's a great shame because, on the evidence of Psalm 36, he deserves to be much better known beyond the lagoon. It's an absolutely gorgeous piece.

The week running up to the performance was a hectic one. There were the regular Monday and Thursday rehearsals, with an extra four hours in the concert hall – nothing less than the Scuola Grande di San Rocco – on the Friday night; and a final *prova* two hours before the concert on Saturday. But it wasn't just the music that needed to be sorted out, oh no . . .

Dress code for this sort of thing in the UK is straightforward: evening dress (or *uno smoking*) and bow tie. Not in Italy. In fact, they find the idea amusing, as if the Brits still dress as if they were in *Downton Abbey*. Gianfranco once told me he bought a *smoking* thirty years ago and has worn it twice. Dress code – for the men at least – turned out to be more complicated. On Monday, we were told to wear black trousers, black shirts and the regulation orange tie. On Tuesday, this had changed to a black suit and white shirt. By Wednesday, the black shirt was back in vogue; and by Thursday it was being matched with a black jacket. At the rehearsal on Friday everybody decided it was too hot to wear a jacket, so black trousers, black shirt and orange tie it was. This meant that, should anybody have needed to go out and buy any of the elements, they had half a day in which to do so. This might explain why Max wore a striped blue shirt on the night and Stefano turned up in his jeans.

I had to fight the impulse to laugh out loud at the absurdity of it all. An ex-computer programmer from Swansea, singing a work by an obscure Venetian composer in a room full of Tintorettos? This was insane!

The concert was practically sold out. Seven hundred seats, nearly all taken, a good result on a night that had a number of rival concerts throughout the city (it was the first performance of the Marcello in modern times, which helped). Usual protocol for classical concerts is to give the audience the 'difficult' piece first and finish with something less challenging (the musical equivalent of a reward for eating your greens); but the Bernstein is extremely hard on the voice and had to be last. Marcello was first, then Bernstein, with an encore of the final chorus of the Marcello to send everyone home with a warm glow.

It all went well and everyone seemed pleased. There was a party afterwards, much wine was drunk and enormous pizzas were consumed. People were keen to ask me what I thought of the concert, about singing in such an extraordinary space and what a shame it was that I didn't get to wear my *smoking*. It was another occasion in which I felt that little bit more at home.

Caroline was still up when I got back. She thought we sounded wonderful and that the Marcello was lovely.

'And the Bernstein?'

'Like being hit around the head with a sock filled with wet sand.'

I shrugged. Fair enough, it's a piece that divides people.

'But it's fantastically exciting to sing,' I added, and launched into *LA! MA! LA MA! Lamah rag'shu … lamah rag'shu goyim, lamah rag'shu?*

I saw her pained expression, and stopped.

'Too much?'

She nodded.

And that, you understand, is the reason why I don't sing at home.

Caroline returned from the market with a bag of small crabs, or, to give them their Venetian name, *masanette*. Remember the soft-shelled *moeche*? These are the same, only later in the season, all female and tooled up with hard shells and proper claws.

They were a more active bunch than the soft-shelled guys. I gave them a rinse under running water and within seconds three of them had made a break for it, over the edge of the sieve and into the sink. I plopped them back into, shall we say, 'the waiting room' with the aid of a teaspoon: they may have been small, two inches across at most, but their claws were big enough to get an 'Ow!' out of our fishmonger when she bagged them up.

The recommended cooking method is to put them in a pan of cold water and bring it to the boil. I wasn't happy about this (I don't imagine the crabs were over the moon either) but it seemed to dispatch them quickly, before the water became properly hot.

Then the real work began. I took the first crab, removed the legs and claws, levered off the top shell and painstakingly excised the 'Dead Men's Fingers' with my smallest, sharpest knife. I repeated the process for the other two dozen or so. I laid the halves on a plate and dressed them with salt, pepper, lemon and parsley. The mixture of the deep red-bronze crab shells, the bright yellow roe and the green of the parsley made for a very pretty dish.

What do they taste like? They're quite nice, but there's such a tiny amount of meat to be winkled out of the shells that I'm not sure the ratio of 'Eating Pleasure' versus 'Amount of Arsing Around' is worth it. They needed to be tried, but I wasn't sure I could see them becoming a staple.

I volunteered to do the weekly shop the following week. Caroline had built up a relationship with the people at the Santa Marta farmers' market. She'd become known as *la professoressa,* but, for the time being, she was simply *la signora Scozzese.* She isn't Scottish, but explaining the complexities of British national identities is tiring when you have to explain it to everyone you meet.

I went along to the butcher's stall to collect the liver she'd ordered. The *signora* recognised me as the husband of the Scottish woman, and went off to look for it. She came back with a hefty bag.

'How much did you want?'

'Hmm, three hundred grams, maybe four hundred?'

She heaved the bag on to the scales. It was well over a kilo and a half.

'Too much?'

'Erm, well it is really. Just a little.'

She shrugged, 'OK, no problem. Pay for four hundred grams, we'll give you the rest.'

I walked away with a salami and one and a half kilos of liver, for eight euros in total.

I set myself to work as soon as I got home. There aren't many ways of cooking liver other than flash-frying it, and most recipes seem to be variations on:

Liver with onions.
Liver with wine.
Liver Surprise (liver without onions or wine).

I failed to find any that recommended 750 g per person, so this all needed to be packed away into the freezer. I took a look inside the bag. It seemed to be an entire pig's liver. The butcher had said it was fresh and he wasn't kidding. It was also bloody. After five minutes work my hands, my knife, the chopping board and the surfaces were soaked in blood. The kitchen looked like party night, chez Hannibal Lecter.

I wondered how I would explain it if somebody came to the door and drew unfortunate conclusions from my appearance, the absence of Caroline and a suspiciously well-stocked freezer.

Liver freezes very well and *fegato alla veneziana* – with white wine vinegar and onions – is a local speciality. I could see it becoming a staple over the coming months.

Early one Wednesday morning, earlier than I'd been used to for some time, I stopped off at my regular newspaper stand, stuck my copy of *Repubblica* into my laptop case and walked to Rialto. It was quiet, hardly anyone on the bridge yet, but the vaporetti were starting to fill and I found myself sitting among a group of excited Japanese tourists. I read my paper and refused to look at the view as we made our way up the Grand Canal. This was silly, obviously, but I was making a statement: *I can look at this any time, but right now something important is going on in the world that I need to know about. I am not on holiday, I am going to work, just like any ordinary Venetian.*

I was pleased at having secured some work teaching Business English in Venice, although it was a little deflating when it turned out to be in Tronchetto, a part of the city so resolutely un-magical it even has cars. It was convenient to travel to, so I couldn't complain. The job had come out of the blue so I hadn't time to be nervous: *Can you take over from another teacher? Great. Can you start on Wednesday . . . no we don't have anything to hand over to you . . . sorry, but you'll have to wing it for the first lesson or so.*

The hours passed with no disasters. Everyone seemed pleased and I even managed to enjoy it. I made my way back to the vaporetto stop, took a coffee in a local bar and read more of the paper. I stopped off at the Rialto market on the way home and picked up four *seppie* for tea, a bargain at a couple of euros. I noticed the water was higher than it had been for a while and some of the *calli* were starting to flood; a sign that autumn was coming.

I hopped on the next boat, bag of cuttlefish in one hand and laptop in the other. This time, I looked at the view and – at that moment – felt more than ever that I truly belonged here.

Let's take a bit of time – in case you decide to do something like this yourself – to look at the education system in Italy, both private and public, and how you might go about finding work.

The state education system in Italy (and education is almost entirely state-provided) runs through the stages of *asilo* (nursery), *elementare* (6–11 years), *scuola media* (11–14) and *scuola superiore* (14–19). *Media* and *superiore* are the ones most likely to be of relevance to a CELTA-qualified teacher. Education is of a high standard, and English is compulsory from *media* onwards. In a country with a high level of youth unemployment, many parents are keen for their children to have additional classes outside of school as well.

At the end of *scuola media*, pupils (or students, as you'll learn to call them) get to choose a general area of specialisation – languages, arts, classics, sciences, etc. – which governs which sort of *scuola superiore* they go to. This tends to impact on the gender balance of classes and, also, on the level of interest in English. This is not something over which you have any sort of control, but be aware that the 'liveliness' of the class is likely to be different between a 90 per cent female class in a human sciences *liceo* and a 90 per cent male class in an *istituto tecnico*.

The school day is usually 8 a.m. until 1 p.m. or 2 p.m., and it's not uncommon for classes to be held on Saturday morning. Christmas holidays are about two weeks, Easter not much more than a long weekend. There is no half-term. By way of compensation, there are frequent public holidays and the summer break is almost three months in length. The downside is you will most probably not be earning anything during that period.

One more thing: it is possible for a student to have to repeat an entire year if their end-of-year grade is deemed insufficient. Prepare yourself for the possibility of a bearded six-foot youth towering over the rest of your second-year *scuola media* class.

Your employment is likely to be with a private language school who will use you to provide lessons for groups of both adults and children, as well as exam preparation classes, Business English and sending you out to work in the state system as a *lettore*.

A *lettore* is somewhere between a teaching assistant and an actual teacher in that it is your responsibility to deliver the lesson – in English – while a qualified Italian teacher remains in the class with you (for reasons of insurance, and to maintain discipline). At its best – if you have a nice class, and a good relationship with your co-teacher – the position of *lettore* can be extremely rewarding. It can actually be better than being a teacher, in that you get to do the fun bits of teaching – the actual teaching – while ignoring the attendant bureaucracy. Once you have a few years' experience under your belt, you can apply for these positions directly – at the outset, however, it's most likely you'll be gaining this experience via a private language school.

Do you actually need a CELTA in order to find work? Not necessarily, but it will help. You might find a private school willing to take you on without one, but you will find it enormously difficult to find work in the state system.

A word on language schools. Be very careful. None of them are going to pay you enough to become rich, but the good ones will pay you legally (i.e. into a bank account with deductions for national insurance that will allow you to access health and social security services), on time and perhaps with a few perks such as overtime or payment during the summer months when the school is closed. The bad ones will make you fight for every cent you've earned. The most drastic case I know concerned a teacher turning up for work one morning to find the school closed down and the owners nowhere to be seen. More common is to find yourself trapped, after a few months of empty promises of imminent payment, wondering whether to give the whole thing up and write off the money or to stick it out, effectively working for nothing, in the hope that some money will be forthcoming. If you're going to work for a language school you *must* do your research beforehand.

We started by emailing every private school we could find on the internet. We had no real knowledge of the education sector and had to big up our 'life experience' in the hope of making our wafer-thin teaching CVs appear more impressive than they were.

Most of these emails went unanswered. A school in Treviso replied, but lost interest when they found we were living in Venice. The travelling, they told me, would be too difficult for us. I had naively assumed that we would be working a standard nine-to-five day. It wasn't going to be like that – work would be split between morning sessions in schools and evening sessions for adult learners. I should have thought of this – there is, after all, a reason why 'evening classes' are called 'evening classes'.

This made it more difficult than expected. I had thought it would be straightforward to commute from Venice to Treviso or Padua. I now realised this wasn't going to be possible.

Caroline found some paid work at a small place on the Lido. She started with two Ukrainian women, one of whom spoke some English and the other some Italian. After the first lesson, one of them demanded to be taught in Italian. After the second, the other demanded to be taught in English. There was no third lesson and the pair went on to burn out another three teachers by Christmas.

This was a stroke of good fortune, however, as within a couple of weeks Caroline found herself employed by a reputable school in Mestre.

By now the two of us were working almost a full week. Once a week, I taught two IT workers from the electricity supply company ENEL on Tronchetto. Three times a week, I would teach staff at the Holiday Inn in Marghera with varying degrees of success. The staff were nice, but seemed baffled why I was there as most guests came from South America or Russia.

I also had some individual students. A keen-as-mustard water-taxi driver; a nice lady who worked at La Fenice; an architect working on the Hotel Excelsior; and a lovely bloke who ran a fine art restoration business and who wanted to spend his second lesson discussing a short story by Chekhov.

And there was the Honorary Consul, an Italian businessman who acted as consul on behalf of citizens of a country in South-East Asia. I would turn up at his office every Thursday, equipped with a lesson plan that was rarely used as there would usually be some consular business that he needed my help with, in my capacity as an English speaker, a language that served as a *lingua franca* for tourists that might not speak Italian. Every week, people seemed to be contacting him with a different set of problems, from lost passports to malfunctioning iPads. What a very interesting job that must be, I thought . . .

Caroline, by contrast, had to deal with classes full of shouty, hyperactive Italian teenagers, hopped up on a deadly cocktail of caffeine, e-numbers and hormones.

I considered myself fortunate to have avoided this fate until the same language school offered me a contract in nearby Spinea. It was a few hours a week, but with the possibility of something more substantial and, if I did well enough, a full-time contract for the following school year. The position involved teaching *scuola media* children for a couple of hours on Monday and Friday afternoons.

I went for a chat with the director of studies, an amiable Leeds United supporter with a penchant for obscure films and even more obscure rock music.

'So, it's basically being a teaching assistant?' I asked.

'Erm, not exactly. You see, the school day finishes at 1 p.m. You'll be taking after-school classes on your own.'

'Hang on, you mean there's not going to be an actual teacher there *at all*?'

'No, just you. But they should be fine. After all, they want to attend because they've shown an aptitude for English. Apart from the ones who've been told they have to go because they're lagging behind.'

I gulped. For a moment I considered saying, *There seems to be some kind of misunderstanding. I think the person you're looking for is a teacher. I'm a failed IT professional. In fact, I'm a failed IT professional who doesn't like children very much.*

And then I thought 'No job too small' had been a good motto, but 'No job too terrifying' was an even better one.

'Sounds great,' I smiled.

*   *   *

My two Business English courses came to an end. The guys at the electricity board were very pleased. The staff at the Holiday Inn were sympathetic. I'd done my utmost, but it had been an uphill struggle. The best of them, Luca, a waiter in his thirties, had turned up late, unshaven and hungover for his final test and had made a terrible mess of it. He looked stressed and unhappy, and I asked him what was wrong. His boss, he said, was angry with him.

'Why's that?'

'Two customers in the restaurant called him over. They said I'd been rude to them.'

'Ah, sorry to hear that.'

'So I said to them, "F**k you man, I was not rude to you!"'

I paused.

'Luca . . . maybe it's different in Italian . . . but in English, that is kind of a *bit* rude.'

Business English was not something I was desperate to do more of. The after-school classes in Spinea, however, were turning out to be great fun. Completely against the odds, working in schools was what I enjoyed the most.

I had thought my timetable was going to be thin by the end of the year, but work kept flooding in. So much so that the logistics were becoming complicated. A typical day might start with a class on the Lido, following which I'd catch the boat to Piazzale Roma and then the bus out to Spinea for the afternoon, stopping off in Mestre for an evening class. If ACTV had operated a 'boat miles' scheme, I'd have been coining it.

We were almost at the limit of the hours that we could realistically work. We were aware that it might not always be like this and that the summer months were likely to be quiet, but, for the moment, it was a nice problem to have. Our dining-room table had become a repository for *Headway*, *Cutting Edge*, *New English File*, *In Company*, *Business Focus*, *Practical English Usage*, *The Practice of English Language Teaching* and the blessed Jim Scrivener's *Teaching English Grammar*; as well as books full of phrasal verbs and ten-minute filler exercises for those awkward moments when you look at the clock and realise you're going to under-run.

It was turning out to be a most unusual job. In the same week I prepared two hours of business material (inevitably unused) for the Honorary Consul, a lesson on the restoration of Jan van Eyck's *The Annunciation* (the art restorer wanted to learn some technical vocabulary before delivering a series of lectures at a university in Yemen, a location he casually described as 'maybe not so safe'), and a lesson for teenagers explaining the magic of the traditional English Christmas via the music of Slade.

A word on using pop music in class. It can work well if you choose the right song. 'Octopus's Garden', for example, is great for the conditional and for prepositions. Also, the guitar solo is really good. On the other hand, you will feel middle-aged when having to explain to a class of thirteen-year-olds who George Harrison was, and the song does have to be something you'll be happy listening to over and over and over again. I played 'Merry Christmas Everybody' three times in each class. I think it will be some time until I need to hear it again.

It was the strangest job I'd ever had. It was almost certainly the best, as well.

Caroline, faced every day with an army of bellowing teen-agers, might not have agreed. She came back from teaching one Friday evening and announced that it had 'not been completely horrible'. It felt like we should crack open a bottle of prosecco.

Chapter 13

I found myself making my way home from a class on the Lido on a wet November evening. It was pitch dark, with a howling wind sweeping in from the lagoon and pushing great sheets of water along the streets. It was only 7.30 in the evening, but there was not another soul to be seen. No one was venturing outdoors. I knew the tiny umbrella in my bag wouldn't last more than a couple of seconds in the gale, so I crammed my hat onto my head and headed for the bus shelter as fast as a man in a pair of wellies can run.

Caroline texted me to say she'd seen tourists on a gondola back in the *centro storico*. The rain was horizontal. You could hardly see beyond a few metres. You would have to be insane to want to go out on the canals. But our Japanese cousins are made of sterner stuff. They'd come this far to have a gondola ride and they were damn well going to have one even if it nearly killed them.

A bus arrived within a couple of minutes and there was a short wait for a vaporetto from Santa Maria Elisabetta. For once, nobody wanted to go and wait on the jetty to be first in line for a seat. Everyone huddled under cover until the last moment. A few young people were in fancy dress, on their way to a Halloween party. I hope it was worth it. It would have needed to be the best party in the world.

I squelched into the flat forty minutes later. Our landlady had been round to put a new seal on the *paratia*, which now seemed to be properly chocked into place. Caroline, bless her, had been cooking, and a steaming risotto of gorgonzola and walnut, with copious quantities of wine, soon had me feeling human again.

There was no point going out in this, so we had an early night. There was a code red warning for *acqua alta* with the peak, at midnight, predicted at 140 centimetres above average. Our street was still flooded the next morning; the water levels kept high by a combination of the phase of the moon, the incoming scirocco and a lagoon already swollen by days of rain.

I needed to go out and buy a loaf of bread. It was the first of November – *Ognissanti* or All Saints' Day, a public holiday – and the city was quiet. I splashed my way to Campo Santo Stefano and along the *passerelle* to the supermarket where, for a few minutes, everything seemed normal. Then back outside, to the flooding, pedestrians in disposable waterproof boots and shopkeepers running pumps or sweeping out the pools of water as best they could.

Venice had remained relatively unaffected by *acqua alta* during the previous year, the water level rarely exceeding 110 centimetres above the average. This, however, was the most sustained flooding for nearly fifty years. A third of the city was affected for fifteen hours, the longest period since 1966.

The water levels have been higher in the past. Ominously half of the highest recorded levels have occurred in the past decade. The MOSE project is supposed to help – great submerged gates that can be raised to isolate the lagoon in the event of exceptionally high waters – but nobody is convinced by this and there's no sign of it being finished any day soon.

You might have seen pictures on television of tourists 'swimming' in Piazza San Marco. If you've walked through the piazza and seen what tends to litter it, you might think twice about walking barefoot, let alone swimming. I hear they can do marvellous things with antibiotics these days.

From the news reports in the UK, you might have assumed that something apocalyptic was happening. If you spoke to local people, the reaction was more phlegmatic: wear wellies and don't go near Piazza San Marco. It wasn't 'chaos', it wasn't a 'disaster' and Venice is not about to slip beneath the waves.

The reality is that you couldn't *really* swim in the piazza. The water was deep, but not deep enough. The serious problems were not in Venice but elsewhere throughout northern Italy. Three electricity workers were killed when a bridge collapsed in Grosseto. Sadly this was never going to be as newsworthy as an image of tourists sitting in their swimming costumes outside a café. It's November. It's cold. For God's sake put some trousers on.

Winter had arrived. The blazing heat of August and the weeks of oppressively bright blue skies were memories. It was bitterly cold, the kind that sinks deep into your bones. It was hard to imagine that three months previously it had been too hot to sit outside.

I liked that it was hat, coat and scarf weather again. I liked the streets quiet and shrouded in thick blankets of fog. Piazza San Marco was no longer a no-go area. I could almost forget that I owned such a thing as a pair of shorts.

Winter suits me and those few weeks were perhaps my happiest since we arrived. There is no more enthralling city than Venice at night and I would choose a different route home whenever I returned from work, wandering the foggy, semi-lit *calli* where the only sound was my own footsteps.

What a chap needs to look the part on a cold winter's day is a *tabarro*. This is a type of Venetian cloak (and also the title of the shortest and nastiest of Puccini's operas). For the last ten years, one of the *tabarrifici* in Venice has organised a *Gran Liston* in which lovers of the *tabarro* take a stroll through the streets, cloaks a-swinging.

We tagged along for part of it, beginning in the Piazza. There was the occasional break for a song and a certain amount of capering, if not all that much to see. It was a good excuse for a walk and the *tabarro* and hat combination is a striking one, even if the preponderance of grey-bearded men gave the impression of having wandered into a fancy-dress party where everyone has come as Vincent Price in *Witchfinder General*.

It's a shame that people don't wear cloaks any more, but – unless you're a vampire or a masked crimefighter – it's a difficult look to carry off. If there's anywhere in the world where it still has its place, it has to be Venice on a foggy winter's day.

I would very much like a *tabarro* of my own. The trouble is they seem to be handmade and price on application. For the time being, along with a hat by Borsalino, it would have to go on the wish list.

Christmas in the UK begins around October and three months of 'Be of Good Cheer, By Order' is wearisome. It's more low-key in Venice. Nothing much starts until December and lights and decorations only go up with a couple of weeks to go. It feels less commercial and less like hard work.

The windows of *cioccolaterie* filled up with ornate displays. Legendary wine shop, bar and *cicchetteria* Al Bottegon (a place we've been coming to since 2005, and where we have built up a relationship with the staff to the level where we sometimes get a half-smile) had its usual tree constructed of wine corks. *Presepi* started to appear in churches. The Venetians are keen on these: nativity scenes, from the Latin *praesepium*. They go to extraordinary lengths in their construction. The one at San Trovaso contained two water features, fire effects and clever lighting that cycled from dawn to dusk to the dark of night. The Scalzi was in full-blown 'art installation' mode where the visitor encountered life-size magi in an alcove on the right, from where the gaze was drawn up to a great, golden comet-like strip that led across the vault of the roof to the Holy Family in the chapel opposite. Not to be outdone, the Frari attempted an immersive experience with an outdoor 'living *presepio*' with all the characters played by local children. At least that was the idea. Whenever we passed, the *bambini* were conspicuous by their absence. I suppose if the contest was between sitting outside for hours in the cold and damp pretending to be a shepherd or staying at home with the Xbox, there was only likely to be one winner. *O tempora o mores.*

Santa Maria Maddalena hosted its twenty-second *Mostra del Presepio*, which provided an opportunity to have a look around a rarely open church. The sheer number and scale of the scenes all made it difficult to get a proper impression of the interior, but there was the chance to see a Last Supper by Giandomenico Tiepolo. Many of the *presepi* show biblical scenes transferred to a Venetian setting: a Doge pays homage to the Holy Family in a stable positioned in front of the Rialto bridge, as gondolas pass in the background.

Some of these might appear naive or kitsch, but conceptually they're no different from religious art through the ages, where biblical scenes were set against contemporary and local backgrounds, and the great and the good had themselves painted as participants in the drama (either for egotistical reasons, or in the hope of scoring bonus points when it came to the immortal soul being weighed). They're some of the most delightful Christmas sights to be seen in the city.

The Cantori's seasonal concert was held two days before Christmas. It hadn't been long since the Marcello/Bernstein performance and so was more modest in scale. It was an interesting programme – two Magnificats from Arvo Pärt and Herbert Howells respectively, and Gustav Holst's 'Christmas Day'. Nothing in Italian, which put me in the strange position of general source of advice on pronunciation and translator of archaic English words.

The venue was the island of San Lazzaro degli Armeni. There's been a church here since the twelfth century, when the island served as a quarantine station and leper colony. After falling into disuse it was gifted to the Mechitarist order of the Armenian Catholic Church in 1717. It was the only monastery to be spared when Napoleon abolished the other institutions in 1810. After almost three hundred years, this tiny spit of land remains one of the great centres of Armenian scholarship.

Lord Byron spent much of 1816 here, rowing to the island every day to talk with the brothers and learn about their culture and history. Not only did he learn the language, but he also compiled a grammar, contributed to a dictionary and translated various episodes from the Bible. Given that he managed to do all this while finding time to write poetry and enjoy adventures of a 'Byronic' nature, why was it taking us so bloody long just to learn Italian?

It was a cold and foggy day so – though Byron would have been appalled – the vaporetto was the easiest way to get to the island. It wasn't much warmer in the church. It's a beautiful, jewel-like interior and a lovely space in which to perform.

Good wishes were exchanged, sparkling wine was drunk and ridiculous amounts of panettone were consumed in the refectory afterwards; then it was time to head back to Venice. Feeling, once again, that bit more at home.

Christmas Eve was a mixture of British radio ('Nine Lessons and Carols' and *The Archers*; just typing that made me feel old) and Italian cooking. Our fishmonger told Caroline that the traditional Venetian meal for Christmas Eve is risotto of *volpina*, followed by roast eel, so that's what we had. *Volpina* is one of the many words the Venetians have for grey mullet and it makes for a very fine risotto – a little plain, perhaps, but if you're following it up with an eel, that's all to the good. I've never enjoyed eel much before (and the icky method of dispatch that Mr Eel undergoes at the hands of the fishmonger did little to encourage me), but roasting it in a hot oven for thirty minutes was the way to go – the flesh was meltingly soft, the skin deliciously crisp.

Christmas dinner was thoroughly British: a roast goose in marmalade, with sprouts, bread sauce and red cabbage. It took hours of honest toil and sweat by myself, in a kitchen the size of a shoebox, but it was worth every minute. It went well with a nice bottle of red wine that one of my students had bought me.

A year had passed since Christmas in South Wales. So much had changed for us in those twelve months.

My attempt to make toast on the morning of 31 December was scuppered by a cloud of greasy, grey smoke that came pouring out of the oven within seconds of switching the grill on. This shouldn't have surprised me given that it hadn't been cleaned since roasting an eel and a goose on consecutive days.

I had a spray around with the Italian equivalent of Mr Muscle and left it for half an hour. I returned to find the bottom of the oven covered in a thick layer of melted fat. I could feel my arteries hardening just looking at it. Cleaning it out was a less than lovely job, but I gave myself a break by scrubbing out the filter in the dishwasher as well.

We spent the afternoon on prep for next term. I put together a lesson for my students based around Hogmanay in Scotland. I described what a great time people were having in the place we left a year ago, whereas in our new life, we were spending the day working. It seemed terribly postmodern.

New Year's Eve never used to be like this. But it didn't need to be the same. It used to be a final, desperate booze-up at the fag-end of the festive season, as we tried to blot out the horrible reality of going back to work. Now it didn't seem so important. In a week's time, I'd be back at work but I loved my job and I'd be in Venice. And if Caroline loved the job somewhat less than I did, at least she'd be in Venice as well.

There was a party organised in Piazza San Marco, but it didn't sound like our sort of thing. Neither of us felt like standing around for hours in sub-zero temperatures listening to DJs. We settled in for the evening and I cooked the traditional Italian New Year's Eve meal of *cotechino e lenticchie*. *Cotechino* is a sausage consisting of miscellaneous bits of pork, salt, spices and a lot of fat. We'd tried its near relation *zampone* (a stuffed pig's trotter) in the past but found it just a bit too agricultural. There was some Brahms and Mahler on RAI Tre and a pause for the President's Address (the Italian equivalent of the Queen's Speech) halfway through. I was happy to potter in the kitchen as Caroline caught up on her email mountain.

Dinner wasn't much more than OK. You might describe it as 'unctuous', but you'd also move swiftly on to 'a little more unctuous than you'd like'. It was fatty and there was no getting away from the fact that we weren't dealing with prime cuts of meat. We were prepared to give it a go next year, although I thought we should take a step up from Billa's own boil-in-the-bag range. The meal is alleged to be a bringer of good luck and the lentils are supposed to bring money. Perhaps we could just stick with the lentils?

We went up to the *altana* to watch the fireworks at midnight, enjoyable if not on the scale of Redentore. It had been a low-key New Year's Eve, but it didn't need to be anything more. The year 2012 had been the maddest, craziest of our lives. We were allowed to finish it with a quiet night in.

I've always wanted to live within walking distance of an opera house and now we were living five minutes from La Fenice. It seemed so wonderfully civilised. Even more so on New Year's Day, when I could stumble out of bed at 10 a.m., shower, shave, make coffee, have breakfast, fret about what to wear and be at the theatre for curtain up at 11:15.

The first public opera house in the world was in Venice. At one time it had ten of them. La Fenice was built in 1792 on the site of the Teatro San Benedetto, which had burned to the ground, a fate which befell La Fenice itself in 1836. It is one of the world's great lyric theatres. It was the site of premieres by Bellini, Rossini and Donizetti. In the twentieth century, Britten, Stravinsky, Berio and Nono all wrote works for it. But the composer most associated with La Fenice is Giuseppe Verdi, whose *Attila,* *Rigoletto*, *La Traviata* and *Simon Boccanegra* premiered here.

When it burned down again in 1996 (a pair of electricians, involved in a contractual dispute, set fire to it) there was never any doubt that it would be rebuilt. In 1836, it took twelve months. This time eight years were needed. There's a lesson about progress in there somewhere . . .

The entire philosophy behind the reconstruction was *com'era, dov'era* ('as it was, where it was'). And so it is. It's quite an achievement, but whether it was the correct decision is another matter. Opinion on the new Fenice is mixed. It's very pretty but it is a brilliantly realised fake and an opportunity was missed to move away from the image of the 'museum city'. If you were to design an opera house today, you wouldn't start with the traditional horseshoe-shaped system of boxes that leaves half the audience sitting at ninety degrees to the action on stage. *La Repubblica* lamented 'the city should have had the nerve to build a completely new theatre; Venice has betrayed its innovative past by ignoring it'.

It is still a lovely place to go to the opera. The tradition of a New Year's Day concert only dates back to the reconstruction, but the rationale behind it is a good one: given the viewing figures for the New Year event in Vienna, why shouldn't Venice have its own? With the spiky historical relationship between Venice and Austria, why wouldn't a programme of Verdi go down better than a programme of miscellaneous Strausses?

This year, the city had pulled off a coup. The Vienna concert was under the reliable if stolid direction of Franz Welser-Möst, but Fenice had a genuine star in baroque specialist John Eliot Gardiner. It was a surprising choice, as one associates JEG with reverential treatments of Monteverdi and Bach. He didn't seem the type for the light-hearted atmosphere of a New Year's Day concert. Everyone would have been up late. Strong drink might have been taken. We could listen to two hours of Bach and examine our relationship with God and the hereafter, but what we want at 11 a.m. on 1 January are the best bits of Verdi and some stomping choruses to set us up for the year ahead. After a just-serious-enough first half (the *Aida* Sinfonia and Tchaikovsky's second symphony), that's what we got – a selection of Verdi's Greatest Hits.

There was an explosion of glitter at the end and a clap-along to the final 'Brindisi'. JEG isn't usually one to tolerate this sort of frivolity, but he got into the spirit of the occasion and asked the soprano to join him for a waltz on the podium. Everyone left in good humour, out into a cold and foggy Venetian afternoon.

A word on 'restricted view' tickets at La Fenice. These seem to give you a 75 per cent chance of a view of most of the stage without too much craning and a 25 per cent chance of being behind a pillar. On this occasion, Caroline got the pillar. I did offer to change seats, but she insisted. My work in the kitchen over Christmas had built up a stash of Hubby Points. I figured it was time to cash them in.

Chapter 14

I was waiting for a bus home from Mestre when a guy came bounding past, gave me an ambiguous smile, jabbed a finger in my direction and cried *'Lega Nord!'* I was taken aback, and he was on his way without breaking his stride by the time I manage to splutter an *'Assolutamente no!'*

The Lega Nord were the separatist party of northern Italy. Their platform was that the south of the country is corrupt and crime-ridden and everyone in the north would be better off if they were to secede and form an independent state called *Padania*. They had a modest amount of support but enough to have kept them in government, as minor partners of Berlusconi, for much of the previous twenty years.

Opinion on the Northern League varied. Some saw them as an eclectic group of individuals from across the political spectrum who believed that they were so culturally different from the south that the only way forward was separation. Others considered them an unpleasant bunch of neo-fascists. I'm trying to be objective, but given their obsession with an invented past (Padania has never existed except in the broadest geographical sense), weird symbolism (the *Carroccio*, a mobile altar that could be wheeled into battle), a dubious attitude to foreign people (their ex-leader's suggestion that the illegal immigration problem on Lampedusa could be solved if the navy were allowed to open fire on unarmed refugees) and genuine 100 per cent mentalism (their high-profile MEP who expressed support for Anders Breivik and attempted to set fire to a homeless man) . . . you'll understand if I'm erring towards the 'fascist bastards' side.

I have a long bright green scarf that I bought for a St Patrick's Day party a few years ago. Long enough to do that 'folding in two and looping through itself' thing, and not so chunky that it stopped my head moving. It resembled a big floppy cravat. The Northern League is big on green. Green flags. Green shirts. And green scarves . . .

I'm not sure what the man at the bus stop meant. Was he a *Leghista* (in which case, was I supposed to give him a clenched-fist salute?), an anti-fascist (a clenched-fist salute might have been met with a bunch of fives) or, more likely, did he see my scarf and pick up on it for a joke?

I packed it away and pressed another into service. A shame. I was fond of my bright green scarf. But not so much that I was prepared to risk dangling from it.

The Northern League have since rebranded themselves as 'The League', a far-right Italian nationalist party that has come increasingly under fire for alleged racism. At the time of writing, they are currently partners with M5S in Italy's coalition government.

'This chain of solidarity is wonderful: the only way to help us now is to buy parmesan cheese' – Giuseppe Alai, president of the Parmigiano-Reggiano Cheese Consortium

Approximately 300,000 wheels of Parmesan cheese were damaged during the earthquake in Emilia Romagna. They were stacked up in warehouses, where they'd been left to mature. When the earthquake hit, the stacks collapsed and many of the wheels broke open or cracked.

Set against the loss of life and the destruction of property and historic buildings, this might seem trivial, but it wasn't. Parmesan cheese takes years to mature and a warehouse full of cracked and damaged cheeses means your income for the foreseeable future is wiped out.

The producers came up with a solution. If a cheese had been damaged it couldn't be left to mature further, but there was no reason why it couldn't be sold now. Regional associations throughout Italy helped to set up a market for 'Earthquake Parmesan' where consumers could buy perfectly good cheese at a reduced (but not exploitative) price.

We hadn't seen any outlets for it in the city, until Caroline saw a sign outside the local office of the Communist Party. She said she was just on her way to the shops, but I like to think that she drops by every week for a quick chat about Gramsci's theory of Cultural Hegemony over tea and biscuits. She popped in and found herself in a smoke-filled room where the comrades seemed confused by her presence, until she explained that she was there to help in The Struggle and came away with a kilo of cheese.

It was first-class, with that wonderful crunchiness that the best Parmesan has. It lasted for months, but we should have gone back and stocked up with more.

There was a month until the Italian election and, on the evidence so far, the Communists had the best festivals and the best cheese. If we'd been entitled to a vote, they'd have had ours.

Italian politics is complicated.

I was in Rome in 1994, when Silvio Berlusconi won his first election. I didn't know much about him, but what I knew I didn't like. When his government fell later that year I assumed I'd never hear of him again.

Lesson one of Italian politics: never, ever write off Silvio Berlusconi.

Mario Monti's interim government, always unstable, had fallen and an election was due. We were not entitled to a vote, which was just as well. The Italian system – with its raft of parties and coalitions, and a dreadful electoral system commonly referred to as *Porcellum* ('the pig sty') – is Byzantine in its complexity. It took some time to make sense of it because this was more than a simple contest between left and right. There were four main players.

Pier Luigi Bersani's Partito Democratico (PD) – the main party of the *centrosinistra*, in an alliance with Nichi Vendola's Sinistra Ecologia Libertà (SEL) and a number of smaller parties of the left. Bersani seemed a decent bloke if not terribly exciting, but a not-terribly-exciting leader was perhaps what Italy needed. Vendola, proudly gay, Catholic and Marxist, was a more charismatic figure, albeit more popular than his party.

Berlusconi's Popolo della Libertà (PDL) – the *centrodestra*, in a coalition with Roberto Maroni's Lega Nord and a number of small right-wing parties of varying degrees of unpleasantness.

Mario Monti's Scelta Civica – a coalition led by Monti, with support from various centrist parties, technocrats and clever people. His technocratic government was more popular with the markets than with Italians, but there was a feeling that he was a fundamentally decent man, and someone who could be sent to meet foreign heads of state without acting like Peter Sellers in an old Blake Edwards film.

Beppe Grillo's *Movimento Cinque Stelle* (M5S) – an 'anti-political' movement started by Grillo, a former TV comedian. Grillo had charisma to burn and filled piazzas wherever he went, but there remained doubt as to whether M5S was just a weird personality cult, or if it offered anything more than a protest vote for the huge number of voters sick of the current system.

A couple of the smaller parties also deserve a mention. CasaPound is named after American poet and celebrity fascist Ezra Pound. Their symbol is a turtle: swastikas, it seems, are passé. The name translates as 'Ezra Pound's House'. I wondered how scary they could be. The vicar of the Anglican church in Venice lives next door to Ezra Pound's house and he's a splendid chap. The answer is 'very scary indeed' – one of their election posters carried the message 'You have been too tolerant for too long.' Thankfully, they had minuscule support.

Rivoluzione Civile was a coalition of the left headed by the anti-mafia prosecutor Antonio Ingroia, in connection with some reformist/anti-corruption parties, as well as the Communists and the Greens. They seemed an interesting bunch. In the grand tradition of left-wing politics, however, they didn't get on with the other left-wing parties and wouldn't talk to them.

Whatever one may think of Silvio Berlusconi, he towered over Italian politics for twenty years. Even in 2013, by now an old man and mired in controversy (he would shortly be banned from public office for five years), there was still a hardcore who supported him. I once made the mistake of discussing this with my student, the water-taxi driver. Silvio, he told me, protects us from the Communists. Politicians are thieves, but Silvio is a businessman. But what about the criminal convictions? Ah, the judges are all Communists. What about the sleazy sexual allegations? All made by feminists or Communists! Bersani? Communist! Monti? He only cares about the Germans! But Silvio . . . Silvio cares about Italy. At which point, I decided I'd pursued the subject as far as was productive.

The Germans wanted Monti. The French wanted Bersani. The markets would have been happy with either, or both, or anyone as long as it wasn't Silvio. What everybody wanted was stability. And stability, on the night of 25 February 2013, is the opposite of what they got . . .

I sat alone on a late bus from Mestre on election night, listening to a drunk holding court as he told the rest of the passengers how pleased he was that Beppe Grillo and M5S had got 25 per cent of the vote. It seemed hard to believe. Did he mean nationally or in the Veneto? Was my Italian a bit wonky? Or was he just a drunk bloke determined to entertain us on the way back to Venice? I stuck my face in my book and tried to avoid any eye contact with him.

He was, of course, right.

Berlusconi's vote, and that of the Lega, was almost half that of 2008. The trouble was that the PD vote had also declined dramatically. In the end, *Il Cavaliere* did what he had to do: he shored up his core vote and, together with his coalition partners, was able to deny the left a majority.

Bersani never made his presence felt. Berlusconi and Grillo are masters at the communication game and there was a large degree of interest from the press in Monti's campaign. The feeling was that Bersani never attempted to seize the agenda and was happy to sit back and wait for victory to drop into his lap.

Monti cut a diminished figure as a politician instead of a technocrat. Had he really wanted to run? Tellingly, his vote from overseas voters was twice what he received at home.

Grillo seemed to spend much of the post-election period as he had the pre-election period: bellowing himself purple and insulting people. If you stripped away the oafishness and the coarseness, he did have a few reasonable ideas and his suggestion of Dario Fo as President of the Republic was inspired (Fo – eighty-seven years old at the time – unfortunately, but understandably, declined).

There seemed no way out of the impasse, short of another interim technocratic government; and new elections sooner rather than later. Bersani chose the most realistic option: he proposed a broad alliance with Grillo. There were some areas of common ground, at least when it came to political reform. Grillo's response to this was '*You have a face like an arse!*'

The numbers in Parliament made it impossible to elect a President of the Republic and Bersani resigned after the humiliating defeat of his nominee, former premier and EU president Romano Prodi. Finally, outgoing president Giorgio Napolitano agreed to stay on. The eighty-seven-year-old Napolitano, a decent and honourable man, had wanted to retire, but agreed to return on condition that the PD and PDL would provide stability by working together in a grand coalition. If they failed, he warned, he would drag them to account for their failures before all of Italy.

After choir practice one evening, a bottle of prosecco was opened and we shared a bitter toast to *ingovernabilità*. Somewhere on high, Garibaldi must have put his head in his hands and wondered if it had been worth all the trouble.

Italian politics is complicated . . .

Chapter 15

In *Life, the Universe and Everything*, Douglas Adams came up with the idea of an orbiting cocktail party that had been running for so long the partygoers were now the great-great-great-great-grandchildren of the original guests. *Carnevale*, which once stretched to six months of the year, must have felt like that.

It fell into decline from the nineteenth century and was banned by Mussolini, who was never much of a party animal. It was reintroduced in 1979, but today it's a more manageable week-and-a-bit.

We had yet to meet an adult Venetian who could get enthused by *Carnevale*, although this was, admittedly, based on a sampling of four people. *Carnevale*, they said, was once a local event for local people, who would meet up, in costume, for music, dancing, eating and drinking. Nowadays it was no longer for Venetians, the city was too crowded and who would want to spend all that time making a costume just to be mistaken for a tourist?

Costumed people were everywhere. This was sometimes quite effective (a pair of cloaked and masked figures seen in a deserted *calle* made for a pleasingly spooky image) and

Philip Gwynne Jones

sometimes less so (a woman in normal clothes, save for a sparkly mask, at a bus stop outside a supermarket in Mestre). On the vaporetto one evening I found myself standing next to a man dressed as Napoleon; something that, in Venetian terms, is akin to going to a Scotland–England game while dressed as the Duke of Cumberland.

It was interesting but not all that enjoyable. Piazza San Marco, quiet only a few days previously, once again became a seething, near-impassable mass of humanity. The vaporetto services were hard work. Walking the streets was less of a pleasure than it had been. If there is a parallel to be drawn, it's with Edinburgh's Hogmanay, which, in the space of a few years, turned into a mass tourist spectacle that made the centre of town a no-go area for locals. *Carnevale* must be exciting if you have an interest in costume. If you like tricorn hats there is no better place to be in February. But it's not really our thing.

Carnevalaltro, by contrast, is the stroppy younger brother of the main event. It was being held in Campo Sant'Angelo, a few steps from our flat.

As I passed through the campo on my way back from work, I noticed stalls were selling beer, wine, kebabs and things that might have been hats. A '*No Grandi Navi*' banner was draped in front of the main stage. The festival slogan was '*Facciamo la festa all'austerity*' (Let's have an austere party) and the logo was the stylised Guy Fawkes mask from Alan Moore's *V for Vendetta* that had become the symbol of the Occupy movement. There was an alternative, political edge to it; a contrast to the smug, manufactured feel of the official event.

A band was tuning up on stage. Excessively loudly, but this is Venice and I thought it would be finished by nine.

It didn't get going until 10.30. The band was an electric folk/rock group (a bit like the Levellers, if anyone remembers them) accompanied by the drummer from hell. With a steady four-four beat in every song, he didn't have much to do, but, by God, he was going to do it LOUDLY.

It was noisy. Very noisy. Sleep was out of the question, so I wandered back to the *campo* to see what was happening. The band were playing away, the drummer hammering the crap out of his skins as if he was afraid they'd leap up and attack him if he stopped hitting them for more than a second. Behind the main stage was a projection of a recent *No Grandi Navi* demonstration, in which a small flotilla blocked the path of a giant cruise ship until they were removed by police boats and helicopter. The square was full of young people and there was a good-natured vibe.

Its heart was in the right place and we probably weren't the target audience. On the other hand, I had to go to work the next day.

The band packed up long after midnight and the crowd, slowly and noisily, made their way home.

I was somewhat bleary-eyed in the morning but cheered myself up with the thought that it only happened once a year. Reading through *La Nuova*, I realised that it had just been the first night. There were another five to go. Friday was Reggae Night and, again, they insisted on sharing their righteous sounds with us until the small hours. Saturday was Rock Night. Sunday seemed to be put aside for a special Festival of Drumming. On Monday, we practically sobbed with relief as a combination of thick snow and *acqua alta* put paid to the festivities.

La Nuova reported that the event was a big success, even among the locals in the square, although the only person I know in Campo Sant'Angelo is a retired lady whose love for four-hour drum solos has yet to be shared with me.

We'd been hoping the final event might be an Acoustic Guitar Night, or even a Mime Night, but, as the drums started to beat out their insistent rhythm, we realised our hopes were dashed. After five days of hell, a team of workers arrived to take down the stage and the disturbingly large loudspeakers. I felt an urge to give them a hug, or at least to lend them a hand. Just to be sure.

Schools get time off for *Carnevale* and half my private students were either off ill or on holiday. There wasn't much work to occupy us but a combination of the weather and the crowds kept us indoors, sulking and eating *fritelle*.

Ah yes, *fritelle*. Or, 'what they don't tell you about the Italian diet'. We'd been grumpy about the festival experience, but there was one good thing that came out of it, and that was the discovery of these little doughnuts. They come in various forms, from the traditional unfilled *Fritelle Veneziane* to varieties filled with pastry cream or zabaglione. When they're good, they're very good indeed. And when they're bad, hell, they're still pretty good. They're only supposed to be available during *Carnevale* and rightly so. Short of giving away free cigarettes, it's harder to think of a greater risk to public health.

We became obsessed with them. No venture outside was complete without a visit to a new shop to work our way through their selection. Every choir practice ended with trays of them being unwrapped and the popping of prosecco corks.

Carnevale came to an end and, sadly, so did our supply of doughnuts. We felt bereft for the first few days, but that was probably our bodies adjusting to the sudden lack of sugar. *Fritelle* are clearly from Satan's own deep-fat fryer but they improved the carnival experience no end. Some Venetians leave the city during the festive period, but that seems excessive. Next year we might stock up on *fritelle*, soundproof the flat and stay indoors for the eleven days.

For all that I loved my job, I found Mondays hard work. I would leave the house at 8.30, returning after 11.00 at night. I wasn't going to complain about too much work but, unfortunately, the weather gods had decreed that Mondays would henceforth be known as Rain Days. It rained all the bloody time that first winter. There are few things more depressing than emerging into the rain from a warm classroom, putting a cold and soggy hat on your head and realising you are still eight hours from a pair of dry socks. There was some relief when it snowed instead, which somehow seemed marginally less wet.

I found myself teaching CLIL classes after Christmas. CLIL, or Content and Language Integrated Learning, is a variation on conventional English teaching in that you teach a subject as well as the language. In the space of a few weeks I taught lessons on apartheid, nuclear physics, the economic crisis and the Italian women's movement – all in English – to Italian schoolkids. It was hard work as it took a lot of prep, but it was both interesting and enjoyable.

Teenagers, I had decided, were good fun to teach. I remembered our CELTA tutor telling me we'd have to teach children, and how the prospect had terrified me. It turned out it wasn't so bad after all. I mean, it's not as if I was having to teach actual infants . . .

Then I landed my dream job – a short-term contract teaching classes in Art History.

The *professoressa* suggested I start with a lesson on Picasso's *Guernica* and use some extracts from Simon Schama's TV series *The Power of Art*. This, I thought, was too ambitious, but I managed to find a version with English subtitles which would help them.

I started by talking about the Spanish Civil War, the Republicans, the Nationalists and Franco. I asked them if they knew who supported the Nationalists. 'Germany,' somebody volunteered.

'Very good,' I said, before adding, *sotto voce*, '. . . and Italy.'

I showed them some video clips. A lot of it was over their heads, but the scenes of the aftermath at Guernica interspersed with images of the painting gave them a general idea.

I started describing each element – *if the horse represents the Spanish people, then the bull represents Franco*. That sort of thing. I moved to the figure in the foreground.

'What's this?'

'It's a man, prof.'

'That's right. Perhaps he's one of the innocent people at Guernica. Now what's this?' I started to think a laser pointer would be really cool, but I did my best with a pen.

'*Una spada*, prof?'

'That's right, in English we call it a sword. What else?'

'It's broken.'

'Good. What does that mean?'

'Defeat?'

'Yes, the broken sword is a symbol of defeat. Now what's this?'

'A flower.'

'A flower – signifying . . .?'

'Hope?'

'Exactly! The figure is next to the sword which signifies defeat and the flower which signifies hope.'

This was going better than I thought. I moved on.

'Now let's look at his arm and his hand. What's this mark in the centre of his hand?'

Silence.

I tried again, 'It's a wound – *una ferita* – in the centre of his hand. What do you think that means?'

Silence.

'OK. Think of religious art. What do we call a wound in the centre of the hand?'

Silence.

Time for Plan B.

'OK then. Where did Picasso come from?'

'Spain?'

'Spain. And where was Guernica?'

'In Spain?'

'In Spain. Now, what religion are the people of Spain?'

Silence.

'Do they have the same religion as Italy?'

Silence.

This was like pulling teeth. The *professoressa* stared at them and shook her head in disbelief.

'What religion are the people of Italy?'

Silence, and then a wavering voice, '. . . Catholic?'

'Catholic, yes! The same as in Spain. So Picasso knew, if he showed an image of a hand with a wound in the centre, people would know what it meant . . . and that is . . .?'

Silence.

I considered adopting a crucifixion pose, but something told me that might be a step too far.

'We would call these marks the *stigmata*. Who does that make you think of?'

Light dawned.

'*Gesu Cristo*?'

'Jesus Christ!' I managed not to shout. 'It signifies the martyrdom of Jesus Christ.'

And so, blessedly, we moved on. Picasso might have thought the symbolism was obvious but he'd never had to deal with a class of thirteen-year-olds.

It was that rarest of Mondays, one that dawned without any prospect of rain. It did bring with it a transport strike (they're not that uncommon over here), meaning restricted hours of service on all vaporetti and buses in the area.

I found myself in Mestre at 8.30 in the morning, for a class that started at 10.15. It was an opportunity for a leisurely breakfast, but you can't really linger over an espresso and a croissant. It was a chance to do some prep prior to lessons starting.

Monday afternoons usually saw me heading over to Spinea for after-school classes, but they'd been cancelled. And there was no point trying to get home, as I'd be needing to head out again as soon as I arrived.

This left me with an afternoon to kill in Mestre. Poor, unloved Mestre. It's not that bad and the main square of Piazza Ferretto – with the cathedral of San Lorenzo and historic clock tower – is lovely. I didn't think that was going to keep me occupied for five hours, however, so I decided to plan my journey home for after my evening class. There are areas of Mestre where you might not want to linger for too long after dark and the tech where I was teaching was a fair way out of town. If I was to walk to the railway station, I wanted the route clear in my mind.

It took a bit of working out, but the only tricky stretch was the underpass near the station. I was probably being paranoid, but, given I'd just picked up my month's pay, I was twitchy about walking around lonely, unlit areas. After a busy March, I found myself with quite a decent amount of cash in my wallet. It would have been a really bad day to get mugged. I consoled myself with the thought that one of my kind students would be sure to give me a lift.

You're all going in different directions then? Nowhere near the station? Not possible to make a short detour? No? No worries, I'll be fine, don't worry about me. Just count yourselves lucky I'm not the one marking your exams.

Off I strode, with as much confidence as a man in a cardigan with a 'man bag' is able. Down Via Miranese. Under the flyover. Towards the station and the underpass. No one else around. Deserted. Or was it? I tried to keep the lyrics of the Jam's 'Down in the Tube Station at Midnight' out of my head as I rounded a scary blind corner, and then

I was up the other side and could see the welcoming lights of the station in the distance. I'd made it. All I had to do was pass through the red-light district that occupies this stretch of road without making eye contact and I'd be nearly home.

The ticket office at the station was closed. As was the newspaper stand that sells tickets for the Mestre–Venezia route. I found a machine but it was out of order. There had to be another one, but there was a train at the platform by now and I was going to miss it unless . . . *oh to hell with it, they never check on this stretch, get on it, you'll be fine.*

I settled into my seat for a read of the paper when a movement caught my eye. A guard was making his way through the carriage, checking tickets. This was, I suppose, inevitable. I'd been working all day, it was pushing eleven and I was going to be fined God-knows-how-much for the sake of a one-euro ticket.

I made my way to the next carriage down, heading away from the guard. And then the next. And the next. I felt like Robert Donat in Hitchcock's version of *The 39 Steps*.

Robert Donat extricated himself from the situation by hurling himself upon an unsuspecting Madeleine Carroll. I glanced around the carriage. The only other occupant was a bored-looking street vendor with a bag full of fake Louis Vuittons. He didn't look like Madeleine Carroll. Even if he had, I thought any sort of hurling would end badly. I continued my way along the train.

The Mestre–Venezia journey takes ten minutes, yet time passed at a glacial pace. We arrived before I ran out of carriages, and I blessed the Italians and their extremely long trains. I felt bad about not paying, but there wasn't an honesty box for me to deposit a euro.

A few people were waiting at the number 2 vaporetto stop as there'd been a sporadic service earlier that evening. A boat home would have been a welcome treat, so I decided to hang around in case. Fifteen minutes later someone official-looking arrived and told us there'd be no more services that night. It had started to rain.

It was a miserable, damp walk home, but I was on the last stretch. Then it turned out there'd been unexpected *acqua alta* and Calle della Mandola was flooded. If I had been thinking straight, I would have realised that there was a stretch of *passarelle* that I could use around the corner, but I wasn't thinking straight. I was, quite successfully, working myself into A Bit Of A State. This was obviously karma. I'd defrauded the Italian train service of a euro and now I was going to have to pay. I rolled up my trouser legs and strode forth . . .

It was 11.30 by the time I squelched into the flat. Caroline was long since asleep. I plopped my soggy socks into the laundry basket and poured myself a large glass of red wine. Next Monday, I told myself, would be better.

Chapter 16

I emerged unscathed from six months of after-school classes in Spinea. The pay, as expected, was nothing to shout about, and the commute could be arduous. Spinea is an anonymous dormitory town of no great interest, probably most famous as the home of champion swimmer Federica Pellegrini. Nevertheless, I had to admit I was having a good time. It was more fun than one-to-one lessons with adults. The job forced me to improvise at times, and allowed me a degree of creativity. The kids were bright, funny and interesting young people. They were also frequently very loud, but I was prepared to let that go. For the first time in almost twenty years, I understood the meaning of job satisfaction.

Caroline's experience was different.

She spent six months working as *lettrice* in a technical high school in Mestre, in classes that were 90 per cent boys. The job frequently reduced her to tears. It was horrible to arrive home full of stories about my wonderful kids only to find she'd been faced with uncontrollable classes with stressed-out teachers who knew the situation was dreadful but seemed unable to do anything about it.

I started to think that the adventure had been a terrible mistake. More than once we would row about it. It took me a long time to work out why it was easy for me and wretched for her. Partly it goes back to personalities: I have always been happy to stand up in front of people. Caroline, less so. If a lesson isn't working, I'll improvise and try almost anything to drag it back on track (shouting only works the first time – after that it is diminishing returns – indeed, getting the *prof* to lose his cool can be seen as a badge of honour in some classes). Caroline plans lessons in meticulous detail – something else that added to a punishing workload.

Almost every English teacher in the Italian state system is female (I have worked with only one male teacher in the past five years). This gave me curiosity value among the students. Caroline didn't have that. In some of the more technical schools, learning English is not a priority among the students and an hour with the *lettrice* can be seen as a chance to skive.

The holiday feeling was over. Venice was becoming like Sighthill, only in a different country. Sometimes the only pleasant part of the day was the late-night vaporetto taking us home down the Grand Canal. And that needed to be followed with late-night cooking and lesson planning, prior to an early start the next day.

We probably had enough money to get back to the UK, but there'd be little margin for error. We had to find a way of making it work.

The long summer holidays gave us a chance for a breather, to rethink what the hell we were doing in Venice, and what we could do to make it easier. There wasn't very much beyond 'keep buggering on and hope things improve'. The long afternoons on the *altana* at least reminded us why we were there.

We needed to decide if we should rent the apartment for another twelve months. Money was tight, but I knew we'd both have full-time work for nine months of the following year. I thought we deserved it. More than that, I thought Caroline deserved it.

Our landlady was amenable. Subject to a year's rent, paid up front . . .

I had never written anything before moving to Venice. Nothing serious, anyway. OK, there had been a couple of articles for student magazines, one of them – 'The Quest for the Hawklords' – being a review of a Hawkwind gig written in the style of Michael Moorcock. I like to think it was better than it sounds. But I had never thought of attempting to write a book, let alone a novel.

The move, I thought, was likely to be the most exciting thing we would ever do, and so I'd kept a blog about it. Whether it were to be successful or not, the experience would be worth recording.

After eighteen months I had one hundred thousand words of text, and forty readers. Self-publishing, via the ebook or print-on-demand publishing, was becoming respectable and stories about self-published authors who'd made a fortune were regularly featured in the press.

I didn't care about becoming fabulously wealthy (although I was not averse to the idea), but I liked the idea of a permanent record of what I still referred to as The Venice Project. I had no idea how to get a book professionally published (hint: start with *Writers' & Artists' Yearbook*) but print-on-demand seemed a practical and no-risk alternative. Surely, I could sell forty books to my readers and more?

I spent the summer putting it together and encountering the downsides of self-publishing: that 'complete creative control' is a synonym for 'doing everything yourself'. It may be different for you – I wouldn't discourage anyone from self-publishing – but for me the fun part is the writing. Proofreading, typesetting, cover design and publicity are very much not.

The book was complete by the time of the new school year. I published it on Amazon, then withdrew it when I realised I had been credited as 'Mr Philip Gwynne Jones' – which made me sound like a Victorian novelist – and put it out for a second time. I waited to see if I could live with the demands of becoming fabulously wealthy.

I needn't have worried. It received good reviews from readers and sold unspectacularly. It was enough to pay for a nice meal every so often and that was enough. It was a record of what we had done and I was pleased with it. I checked its Amazon ranking obsessively for a few months and, as it slid down the charts, I paid it no more mind and forgot about it.

Summer came to a premature end with the news that we were needed to take some exam preparation classes in Mestre. And then we were back into the teaching year.

My boss called me in to talk through my timetable. It wasn't too bad at first sight – mainly evening classes – although I knew work in schools would be coming up later in the year.

We went through the schedule together. Adult evening classes, finishing at about nine, four nights a week. Corso del

Popolo in Mestre is not a lovely place from which to be getting a bus at that time of night, and the commute would mean I wouldn't be home until about ten. The teaching, at least, would be straightforward.

I looked at the slots from five until six-thirty. Each slot on the timetable had a single word.

Bambini.

Four classes a week. Thirty-three weeks.

Bambini.

'One question. These *bambini*, just how, erm, *bambini*-ish are they?'

'Tuesday and Wednesday, I think, are first-year *scuola media*.'

Perhaps eleven years old. I could handle that. 'And Thursday and Friday?'

He grinned. 'They're actual *bambini*.'

'Meaning?'

'*Scuola elementare*. I don't think there's anyone younger than seven.'

'SEVEN?'

'Most of them. Some might be eight.'

'You don't understand. I've not spoken to a seven-year-old since I was, well, seven.'

'You'll pick it up. We've all done it.' He fetched a stack of books from the shelves. 'This is the material we use. Have a read through first. It'll help . . .'

I got home that evening and laid everything out on the table. I made us a pair of spritzes.

Caroline flicked through a couple of books. 'How old are they again?'

'Seven or eight. I've avoided the six-year-olds.'

She gave a hollow laugh. Perhaps for the first time, I started to realise what the experience had been like for her.

I went through the first volume. *Stardust*. The set-up is that two alien children arrive on Earth, accompanied by their robot dog. Hilarious adventures ensue, with comic strips, stories and songs.

I played the accompanying CD, and listened to the 'Up, Up and Away' song that was supposed to begin every lesson.

I cannot do this, I said to myself. *I simply cannot do this. I want my nice art restorer and opera-house lady back. I cannot do this. This is banal, it's silly, it's . . .*

Childish?

But we're talking about seven-year-olds. It's not childish to them.

I played the recording again. And again. I made another spritz. I listened to it once more. And started to think this isn't such a bad tune after all. Maybe it's quite sweet.

If this is what it took to stay in Venice, this is what I would do. I would play the song every lesson, I would sing along, and I would even do the actions.

I was going to need to read stories as well. That shouldn't be too bad. The robot dog, imaginatively called 'Robodog', usually ended up in a terrible scrape in each episode. I tried doing the voice. 'Hello, I'm Robodog.' It seemed to lack something. I tried again, in a falsetto Dalek voice. 'HELLO I'M ROBODOG!'

Much better. On Thursday nights I would sing songs to small children and pretend to be a robot dog. Of course that's what I was going to do.

* * *

I don't know who was the more nervous that Thursday night, me or the kids. I ran through 'Up, Up and Away' in the staff room to reassure myself that I had the actions down pat (in a burst of enthusiasm I'd decided there weren't enough actions and had added some of my own), and perfected my 'Robodog' voice.

I went into the classroom armed with books and official school bags for everyone.

There were six little girls, whose names, I would learn, were Margherita, Giulia, Valentina, Alessandra, Francesca and Very Little Emma (I had a few Emmas that year, and they needed to be distinguished somehow). They stopped talking as soon as I entered the class and stared at me.

I gave them my brightest, warmest smile.

Very Little Emma burst into tears.

Oh.

My.

God.

Come on Jonesy, for the past year you've been telling Caroline how wonderful the job is because you can improvise. So improvise.

A word here on the TEFL methodology. The premise is that you teach English, in English. You do not use the native language. There are good reasons for this: students, especially kids, will start to use it as a crutch once they realise you speak their language.

Nevertheless, six little girls who – in all likelihood – had never had a male teacher before were staring at me. A big, tall, old and, above all, foreign bloke was speaking to them in a language they didn't understand.

It must have been strange.

It was almost certainly frightening.

To hell with the methodology.

I sat on the floor, cross-legged, next to Very Little Emma. I was still taller than her. I spoke to her in Italian. 'Hey, come on. It's OK. This is going to be fun.'

She was, bless her, trying to be brave but the tears were still flowing.

I put the book on her desk, and turned to the first page, with the words to 'Up, Up and Away'.

'We're going to sing a song. I've got a bag for you as well.'

The girls, as one, turned to look at me.

I went back to my desk, and ripped open the box of bags.

They descended on them in a cloud of shrieks, laughs and whirling limbs.

Few things, I realised, were as attractive to seven-year-old girls as the prospect of free things. And a free bag, that was even better, wasn't it!

I took a deep sigh of relief. The air was full of the chatter of excited little girls but that was progress.

I wrote my name on the board, and smiled. 'My name is Philip, and now we're going to sing a song . . .'

Chapter 17

School progressed, and late summer turned into autumn and autumn into winter. It seemed impossible, in the middle of November, to think that only three months ago I had been wondering if I would ever be cold again.

Work was busy but lessons were still confined to evenings. It left us most of the day free, although much of that seemed to be taken up with shopping, lesson planning or preparing something that could be stuck in the oven for a late dinner. But there were some public holidays to break things up, such as the *Festa della Salute*. A day off, and a long weekend, and time to relax.

While I was making coffee, Caroline called out from the bathroom wanting to know why there was no hot water.

I put down the Moka, and took a look in the cupboard. The pilot light had gone out. I pressed the button to relight it, and a comforting WHUMPH came from the boiler.

I closed the door, and shouted that it was all right now.

I heard a hiss of the shower running, and a brief scream told me that, in fact, things were not all right.

I opened the cupboard again and took another look. The pilot light had gone out again.

Oh hell.

La Festa della Salute is not the ideal day to find oneself in need of a plumber. I took a telephone call from one who talked me through how to restore pressure to the boiler. Success! For about thirty seconds. Followed by an ominous KERCHONKATACHONKATACHONKATA sound. He advised me to bleed all the radiators. I did so. Three times. I discovered ones I didn't know we had. Nothing good happened.

He came round on Saturday morning, looked the boiler over for perhaps thirty seconds and told me that, in technical terms, it was knackered. He phoned our landlady and explained they might be able to start work by the end of the following week. No, they couldn't do it any quicker. If there were children or elderly or infirm people in the house, they might be able to speed things up but – and at this point he stared at me for a few seconds longer than I thought necessary – that didn't apply in this case.

He had his mobile phone on speaker, so that I could listen to the conversation.

'So what will need to be done?' she asked.

'*Signora*, in all honesty, it needs to be replaced.'

'I see.' She paused. 'How much might that be?'

'Perhaps three thousand, four thousand euros.'

She paused again. 'Is it not possible to repair it?'

'*Signora*, I have the documentation here. The boiler is nearly fifteen years old. You would expect it to need replacing by this time.'

'I see. Can you put Mr Jones on the line?' He passed me the phone. '*Ciao*, Philip, I am sorry, so sorry for the inconvenience.'

She continued to apologise. Yes, of course if need be she would replace the boiler but given it was a substantial amount of money, perhaps she could try another repairman first? After all, we'd been told we'd need to wait a week until a new one could be installed. Surely it would make sense to get a second opinion?

I conceded that there might be some sense in that. Besides, she'd always been straight with us in the past, hadn't she?

'Of course, *signora*, we'll wait for another *tecnico* on Monday.'

'Thank you, Philip. *Grazie caro*.' I could almost hear her smiling down the line. What a nice lady, I thought.

This left us facing the weekend in temperatures that plunged below zero during the night with no source of heating. We borrowed a two-bar electric fire from the Anglican church in the hope we could keep one room warm. The trouble is, the entire flat – spread over three floors – was open plan. The only room that could be closed off was the bathroom, and given the lack of hot water we were unlikely to be spending much time there.

On Monday, a different plumber arrived and managed to restore a modicum of heat and hot water to the kitchen by cranking up the pressure to a possibly inadvisable level. He gave me a stern warning not to turn the heat up for too long or it would pack up again. Or worse. And he had restored some heat to the kitchen, in that the hot tap produced a terrifying high pressure stream of hissing, bubbling, scalding water. No radiators were working, but the hot water bottle would be better than ever. I called our landlady again. *Signora*, perhaps this time you could come out?

Of course she would, she'd be very happy to. There was one thing. Could she have a third opinion, in case? And Tuesday would be difficult. Perhaps on Wednesday?

The intense cold seemed to be doing something to my perception of the flat. It wasn't that it felt cold, it actually *looked* different, as if all colour had been leeched away and we were existing in a permanently grey environment. And at this point a friend took pity and invited us to stay. I honestly don't know what we would have done without her.

Our *padrona* came to see the situation for herself, in the company of yet another plumber. He took a look at the boiler and the pressure gauge before yanking the dial as far to the left as he could manage. He whistled, and shook his head. '*Pericoloso. Molto, molto pericoloso. Signora,*' he explained, 'this boiler is never going to work again. You must have a new one.'

I don't think she stopped smiling. Of course. As soon as possible. This Friday? *Perfetto.* Philip, would it be OK for you to be here at the same time? To make sure they keep everything tidy.

I turned up on Friday morning, in the company of two plumbers. I didn't think it was possible to get any colder, but the existing boiler had been removed the previous day leaving a nine-inch circular hole in the outside wall.

It took six hours to instal the new boiler. It was bitterly, punishingly cold and I sat with the two-bar fire six inches away from me keeping my left foot warm but little else. I worked on lesson plans, worrying that if I stopped typing I would lose all feeling in my hands.

And finally, blessedly, with a great WHUMPH the new boiler burst into life. I could almost see the colour returning to the room before my eyes. It had wiped out a much-needed holiday weekend but it was done.

The two *tecnici* were scrupulous about cleaning up after themselves. At least our landlady would be pleased, I thought.

Fog lay heavy on the city, and – cold but happy – we arrived home from pre-Christmas drinks with friends. A couple of days more work and the schools would break up and – assuming we could find our passports in the chaos of the spare room – we'd be heading to the UK for a week.

We needed to use up what remained in the fridge and vegetable rack so dinner was potato and celeriac mash, roasted radicchio and some defrosted beef and radicchio burgers from the freezer.

I peeled the spuds, rescued as much as I could from the sad-looking celeriac, and put them on to steam. I chopped the radicchio in half, gave them a generous drizzle with some olive oil, and stuck them in the oven.

I put some Bach on the stereo ('*Jauchzet, frohlocket*') and poured a glass of wine.

I went back to the kitchen and unwrapped the burgers.

I blinked.

The packet did not contain any burgers.

It contained a spleen.

I thought back two weeks. Roberto, at the farmer's market, is a lovely fellow. So much so that – after buying our usual provisions – he had given us a free spleen. There is no greater mark of a gentleman than that. It went into the freezer, in a packet identical to the beef and radicchio burgers.

The radicchio was roasting away happily, and the potatoes/celeriac would be done in about fifteen minutes. Defrosting the burgers was not an option.

I need an emergency spleen recipe, and I need one now.

There was nothing in *The Silver Spoon*, so I checked Fergus Henderson's *Nose to Tail Eating* volumes. There was nothing to be found. And if Fergus cannot help you with offal-related problems, no one can.

I turned to the internet. There were a few recipes, but mainly along the lines of 'first, boil your spleen for sixty minutes' and there was no time. There was a 'rolled spleen and bacon' recipe, but I had no bacon. 'Rolled spleen with no bacon' didn't sound as if it would hit the spot.

I'd only ever had spleen once in my life, at a market in Palermo served in a bun with a squeeze of lemon. I couldn't remember much about it beyond the fact that it tasted like liver and had been quite tasty.

That would have to do. I fried up some onions, trimmed the spleen and sliced it into thinnish chunks and, as soon as the onions had caramelised, into the pan they went. I gave everything a shaking of balsamic vinegar, let it all reduce down, and we were ready to go.

It wasn't too bad. The radicchio had been roasting for a while, but that meant the outer leaves had gone crispy which wasn't a bad thing. As for the spleen, the flavour is milder than liver, although the spongy texture isn't as pleasant. Perhaps that's why the Sicilians serve it in a bun.

Not bad for a free dinner.

*   *   *

It was the Friday before Christmas, which meant beers in the pub over the road from school.

The weather was colder but we sat outside nonetheless for the benefit of the smokers. Hats on, coats wrapped around us. At some point in the next few months the weather would drive us inside, but, for the time being, we were sitting outside a bar on the busy main street through Mestre. We were, in every respect, living the dream.

We were on the second round of beers when a street vendor appeared. He was selling the usual belts, bracelets and necklaces. He told us he was from Senegal. He was polite and friendly and the belts didn't look too bad. But none of us were in the market for anything.

He smiled. No problem. Good wishes were exchanged. Fists were bumped. And then he reached into his bag, withdrew three small elephants and placed them in front of us. A present. He smiled again.

Well, this was splendid!

There was one thing. He was hungry. Could we spare a few euros . . .?

We looked at each other. We looked at our elephants. And, for a moment, the only sound was of three liberal white guys wondering what to do. We reached for our change.

He thanked us and went along his way, heavier of pocket, if lighter of elephants. We called for more beers, proudly regarded our new purchases, and clinked glasses. No more Christmas shopping for us this year!

We wondered if we should leave the elephants on the table as we drank. I thought they might act as a talisman against future vendors who, seeing we'd already made a purchase, would pass us by. Or was it more likely they'd look at us and think, *Ah, the old elephant trick still works?*

We decided to pack them away. I finished my beer and made my way home to Venice. I explained to Caroline that, yes, I was a little bit later than expected, but at least I had bought her an elephant.

Chapter 18

Christmas came and went. Another year had passed, almost without us noticing. We had work, and money coming in, but not enough of it. Savings were slowly being whittled away. A third year in the flat would be impossible – if our *padrona* insisted on a year's rent up front again we wouldn't have the money.

We would need to downsize again. It did seem possible that we could live here long-term, but we'd need to economise. And we'd need some security. That meant getting a place with a guaranteed, long-term lease and one where we could pay monthly and not twelve months in advance. We had contracts now and could demonstrate that we were employed.

The problem was that work was ramping up. In the mornings I worked as *lettore* in Spinea. Three afternoons a week I took after-school lessons there. And I took evening classes in Mestre. It wasn't leaving time for anything other than teaching. Flat-hunting was going to be difficult . . .

The agent fumbled with her keys, but the door opened more easily than expected. It swung open, and a glance confirmed that the lock had splintered from the frame. Somebody had broken in.

She smiled, and looked embarrassed. I smiled back, in a 'well, these things happen' kind of way. We both knew that her job had just become that much more difficult.

The apartment confirmed our suspicions, but she did her best to talk it up. The *terrazzo* floor, in particular, was lovely but once you raised your eyes it was apparent that was all it had going for it. There was plenty of space, but it felt rundown and shabby. There had once been a balcony, but an attempt had been made to glass in the top part and it was held together with masking tape. Half of the balustrade had been covered up with chipboard, with the other half open to the elements. An abandoned exercise bike in the spare room struck a poignant yet threatening note. It was perhaps the most depressing interior space we had ever seen in Venice. Our prospective neighbours appeared to be students on one side and anarchists on the other.

We were not going to spend the next four years here, no matter how cheap it might have been. It was our turn to smile apologetically, and we made our excuses and left.

We needed an unfurnished or partly furnished flat so that, with what remained of our savings, we could start moving our possessions over from the UK. An outside space was non-negotiable. And, again, we were starting to think we'd like to have a cat. All this narrowed our options.

We had almost three months to find somewhere, and people from the choir were keen to help ('We don't want to lose a bass, Philip'). Something would turn up . . .

*   *   *

There is a phrase that I have learned never to use again while flat-hunting: 'You could do a lot with this place ...'

Flashback to 2002, and a place we now refer to as 'the crumbling Gothic pile'. It was a flat in Edinburgh we lived in for two years because I was strangely smitten with its crumbliness. I thought we could do a lot with it. In the end, I fitted a new shower curtain. We moved out shortly after my foot went through the floor and dry rot was discovered ...

One Saturday morning in Castello, I saw somewhere that was a bit rundown, a bit shabby and yet ... with a lick of paint and our own furniture ... surely we could do a lot with it. I reported to Caroline, who went to see it on her own, and returned more in sorrow than anger.

I could hear a sharp intake of breath as soon as I gave the location of the flat. It was still available – the agent explained – but he seemed surprised that there was interest in it.

I looked at my notes.

'It is described as *abitabile*,' I said. Liveable.

'*Abitabile, si.* But in very poor condition.'

'Ah, right.'

'And the building is *un brutto condominio* ...'

'Erm ...'

'... in fact, four people have seen it and said the condition was too bad for them to want it.'

I was impressed by his honesty, although his sales patter possibly needed a bit of work. I was about to sign off politely when he interjected, 'But you should perhaps see it anyway!'

I agreed. I had no idea why.

Caroline headed off to see it the next day. My hopes were not high, yet she returned saying that it was a lot of flat for the money and maybe with a bit of work . . .

'Are you saying that "You Could Do A Lot With It"?'

'I suppose so.'

We made an appointment to see it together.

On a bright Sunday morning we headed off to Giudecca. The agent, an affable fellow who had lived there all his life, met us at Le Zitelle. The building was originally constructed to house workers at the Junghans company. We entered through a locked gate, walked down a passage and through a garden; and past a series of apartment blocks all of which looked in better condition than the one to which he led us.

He told us to be careful as we made our way up the stairs, and gave the bannister a good shake to indicate how perilous it was. The flat was bare. We'd need to get a new kitchen. The bathroom was functional, but a depressing shade of pink, and the plumbing was such that the washing machine drained into the bath.

And yet . . . it was a lot of flat for the money. The location was good, there was a huge amount of space, two terraces (one of which looked out towards the back of the Redentore) and a small (if overgrown) garden.

Then reality kicked in. The place required repainting. The skirting boards, door frames and most of the doors needed replacing. The window fittings were rusting through. Half of the shutters/blinds no longer worked. The floor was in excellent condition but I'm not sure that 'nice floor' is enough of a selling point.

I could, I suppose, have repainted it all myself if I felt like spending an entire baking hot Venetian summer redecorating an un-air-conditioned flat. The rest of it was way beyond me. It could have looked fantastic. It was more likely to be a money pit.

We smiled politely and, again, told the agent we'd let him know.

The search was proving more difficult than we'd thought. I was working six days a week. It wasn't leaving me time to see anywhere and, when I did, the place had inevitably gone. We were running out of time, and I was wondering how flexible our landlady would be about leaving dates.

Nothing was quite right. We were assured that a ground-floor flat near San Lorenzo was *esente acqua alta* – free from flooding – but, given that all the furniture was resting on bricks when we visited, we weren't convinced. An apartment overlooking the Grand Canal near Rialto Mercato sounded too good to be true. It was. The problem was the *movida*, a great bar crawl that passed by every night, generating an unholy cacophony into the small hours of the morning.

We'd seen an advert for a flat near the railway station that sounded promising, and Caroline had the chance of the first viewing. The agent explained that eighty other people had also expressed an interest. This didn't sound beyond the realms of possibility: any number of flats had been taken by the time I'd rung to enquire.

I told Caroline that – if she liked it – she should go for it. If she liked it I was almost certainly going to like it as well. I thought back to 2001 and my decision to spend eighteen months in a crumbling Gothic pile with dry rot. Whose opinion would you trust?

After classes one Friday morning I checked my phone and found a message saying that she'd made an offer and put money down as the first step of the deposit. The agent came back to us saying that the landlord had provisionally agreed. The following week she went along to sign the final agreement.

We got the keys a bit earlier than planned, and I was able to go around there after work one evening. It was behind the church of the Scalzi, near the railway station, in a block originally built for railway workers.

It was not perfect, but we'd realised that nowhere was going to tick every box and this ticked more than anywhere else we'd seen. Truth be told, the only real problem was the kitchen. In fact, it wasn't even the kitchen itself (which was twice the size of our existing one), but the cooker hood and the fridge which the previous occupant had painted an unpleasant shade of yellowy-brown. I was pretty sure I was capable of repainting a fridge. Or, at the very least, I was capable of ignoring it until I didn't notice it any more.

It was done. It had two bedrooms, a bathroom with a proper stand-up shower at last, and a decent-sized living room. There was a balcony that looked over a nicely maintained communal garden, a shared *altana* that looked towards *terraferma* and the mountains on one side, and over to the campanile of San Marco on the other. It was ten minutes walk to Piazzale Roma, which would save an hour of commuting every day, and a short walk to the station in case of a bus strike. We'd been lucky.

And so I had committed to renting a flat for five years without even seeing it. Because my wife is brilliant.

Chapter 19

It took nearly two weeks to get the electricity supply reconnected after the previous tenant moved out. I briefly considered getting in touch with the two ENEL employees to whom I had taught Business English, nearly eighteen months ago, in the hope they might be able to move things along. And then, one evening, I turned up at the flat, flipped the trip switch on the fuse box to the 'on' position, more in hope than expectation, and – the lights came on. I heard the opening bars of *Also Sprach Zarathustra* running through my head . . .

ENI, the gas supply company, refused to believe that there ever had been a gas supply to the flat; but they switched it on anyway. The cooker needed to be connected. The previous tenant had bought a new gas cooker and never used it. Our landlord hadn't known it was there.

Connecting it appeared to be straightforward. I leafed through the instruction manual. Surely even I could manage this? Connect the pipe to the back of the cooker. Switch gas on. How hard could it be? And then I thought about the possible consequences of incorrectly installing a gas appliance. Dozens of other residents. In the middle of an historic city. I shook my head. I badly wanted a cup of coffee . . . but not that badly. Even in Italy, you're not supposed to instal gas appliances yourself. A man had to come out, which took over a week to organise.

It was taking time but the morning and evening commute was much easier. All we needed to do now was arrange the transfer of our furniture from the UK, give our old flat a clear out and get our deposit back. Things were falling into place.

It might seem that I'm giving Italy a hard time when things don't work. I don't mean that. Of course, there are problems: after five years in our current apartment, ENI believe our meter is registered in the name of a woman who died in the 1970s. But when the system works, it works well. And one thing Venice is brilliant at is transporting things by water.

I returned to the UK over Easter to get everything packed up. It seemed a long time since I had been in that shed in the middle of the New Forest, but our furniture (and, not unimportantly, our CDs) had survived intact. It took just a week for our shipment to arrive at the nearest point on *terraferma* to Venice.

We needed to move the existing furniture to the cellar. Most of it could be taken apart with hex keys – nevertheless, some of it was heavy and it was not going to be an easy job for the two of us.

Fortunately, our Brilliant Australian Friends Peter and Lou were on holiday in Venice and, if they had made any plans more exciting than spending a morning disassembling flat-pack furniture, they gave no sign of it. To watch Peter Stockfeld take a hex key to an IKEA wardrobe is like watching Nijinsky dance or Ali box.

The doorbell rang to herald the arrival of the removal men, just as we'd finished stashing the landlord's furniture away downstairs. Within two hours, ours had been installed in its place. It was the most painless move we'd ever experienced. But why should we have expected anything less? The Venetians have been doing this for a thousand years.

We still needed furniture. We had all the essentials but we also had dozens of boxes of books and CDs that needed rehousing if the flat was going to be liveable. It hadn't been worth the expense of transporting cheap bookcases across Europe, so we needed a visit to IKEA, conveniently situated outside Padua.

Why not just order them online? IKEA's delivery charge is a standard rate everywhere in Italy. With the exception, of course, of Venice, where the logistics of delivery require a hefty surcharge. The delivery charge on a standard Billy bookcase is about the same as the cost of the bookcase itself.

Better to get the train and bus to IKEA, hire a van for a modest charge, and bring them back ourselves.

And so we did. We found ourselves in Piazzale Roma, unloading five bookcases onto the faithful B&Q trolley. All we needed was to transport them one stop on the vaporetto, to Ferrovia, and home was a five-minute walk away. There'd be one bridge to negotiate and a few stairs, but it seemed more than manageable.

The *marinaio* told us that we were not, under any circumstances, bringing that lot on board.

We tried arguing. We're residents, we're only going one stop, we'd buy tickets – individual tickets, even – for the bookcases.

No. We were not getting on the boat with all that.

We sat at the base of the Calatrava bridge to consider our options. There was no way we could get five heavy boxes across the bridge by ourselves, and we only had four hours before the van needed to be returned.

There was one thing we could do. We could call our Brilliant Australian Friends again.

'*Pete? It's Philip. It's a Code Red . . .*'

Peter and Lou had probably never envisaged spending a late Sunday afternoon of their holiday hauling furniture across a bridge. But that's what they did.

The logistics were complicated. The weight of the book-cases made it impossible to get more than one across the bridge in one go. And, given we were rapidly running out of time, it seemed unlikely that we could get them all back to our apartment before I needed to head off to Padua with the van.

The solution was for Caroline to stay at the base of the Calatrava bridge, keeping an eye on the bookcases, while Lou waited at the bridge nearest our flat looking after the ever-growing pile of 'almost-delivered' ones. Once all five were on our side of the canal, the three of them would drag the book-cases up to our apartment, while I returned the van.

It worked, but painfully slowly. The round trip from Piazzale Roma to outside our apartment took Pete and I more than thirty minutes for each bookcase. In the meantime, Caroline and Lou baked in the sun watching their respective piles diminish and grow.

Finally, we were done. I left the three of them and scurried back to Piazzale Roma forgetting that, as I was no longer in possession of a bookcase, I was now able to use the vaporetto. Caroline, knowing my lack of directional sense, had scribbled instructions for me on how to get back to IKEA.

I jumped into the van and set off for Padua. I checked my watch. Thirty minutes. That should just about be enough. As I approached the outskirts, I checked directions.

I had forgotten my reading glasses. Caroline's scrawl was indecipherable in the fading light, and there was nowhere to stop on the autostrada.

I barrelled along in the hope that I might see something familiar. I started working on an emergency plan. In the event of not finding the store in time I figured I'd have to find a convenient car park and sleep in the van overnight, returning it the next day, when, hopefully, I would be able to read Caroline's instructions.

I had resigned myself to this when the great yellow IKEA logo swam into view at the end of the autostrada. I checked my watch again. Five minutes. I swung off the road and into the car park, locked the van, and ran.

The store had closed, and staff were cleaning inside. The van hire department was at the opposite end of the building. I ran along outside it, hoping to find an open door. I saw someone cleaning the floors with a buffing machine, and rapped on the glass, like one of the zombies in *Dawn of the Dead*. The cleaner looked up at me and shook her head. I checked my watch again. There was about a minute remaining. I pointed at my watch, shook the keys and pointed towards the 'Van Return' desk. I put my hands together and made a praying motion. Which was not like one of the zombies in *Dawn of the Dead*.

She made her way to me and unlocked the door. I stammered out my thanks and sprinted to the desk.

There was no one there. I saw a box in which to deposit the keys, dropped them in and made my way, unsteadily, to the exit. I'd done it. Now I needed to get home.

There seemed to be just one bus stop in the vicinity, on the slip road coming off the autostrada. It was on the opposite side of the road. I looked around for a bridge or an underpass. The only route seemed to be a looping path that made its way around the outside of the warehouse, through a wooded area to what might have been an underpass perhaps half a kilometre away.

It was dark and the thought of walking along an unlit path and through an underpass did not appeal. I looked across the road to the welcoming, brightly lit bus stop. What time was the last bus anyway? Had I missed it? I had no idea. I started to regret that, having given the keys back, I'd deprived myself of a place to sleep for the night.

Cars sped by, but they were infrequent. I had a reasonable view of approaching traffic, although there was a blind curve in the distance. Surely if I took a good run-up, I could make it across the road?

A lorry whizzed past at high speed, and I winced. Stupid idea. I made my way along the path, through the underpass, up the other side and through another unlit wooded track until I reached the other side of the road. I checked the timetable, and breathed deeply. There would be one final bus in twenty minutes. As I looked back to the opposite side of the road, I noticed a bunch of flowers tied to a lamppost, possibly in memory of the last person who though they might be able to run across the road, and shuddered.

I was the only passenger on a lonely journey back through the industrial estates on the outskirts of Padua. I treated myself to a beer at the station bar, and one at Santa Lucia. Pausing only to get a takeaway pizza, I was home.

The flat was stacked high with packing cases, but I didn't care. It was finished.

It's never good to define yourself by your possessions. Yet, after years of living out of the contents of ten suitcases, there was an inescapable thrill of seeing our CDs, books and art in place again. When the last of the packing cases were cleared we put a record on, propped our favourite painting on a chair and sat, drank wine, and looked at it.

It felt, properly and finally, like our home.

Chapter 20

The end of the school year arrived, and, with it, exams. Well, we called them exams. In the case of the kids it was more of an excuse for a party. They did a test in the penultimate week, and then they'd get an official-looking certificate during the last lesson with their final mark. Something for Mum and Dad to hang on the wall.

The Thursday class had been an absolute delight. Every lesson we sang the 'Up, Up and Away' song, together with actions. They never got bored of it. I'd pretend to be a robot dog, and the girls would laugh as if they'd never heard me doing the squeaky metallic voice before. I discovered that, at the age of seven, the 'Guess the Colour' game (rules – guess the colour on the card, answer yes or no) is the best game in the world and 'Fizz Buzz' is even better, especially if you allow them to stand on the chairs while playing (note to ex-employer – those chairs in Room 3? My fault, sorry).

Brilliantly and unexpectedly I had discovered that – after considering small children to be a different, unintelligible and quite frightening species for most of my life – I was good with kids. Even more incredibly, they seemed to like me. No matter how stressful the rest of the week might have been, my Lovely

Thursday Class (as they were now officially called) would always cheer me up.

They were only seven years old, but they were bright and I was proud of them. Their end-of-year results were as expected. Most of them were in the 90s, but with Very Little Emma a bit behind on 78 per cent. Everybody, I thought, would be thrilled.

And most of them were. There was lots of jumping around, clapping and laughing and comparing of results. Italian kids do this. There's no question of keeping the results to yourself.

Very Little Emma's face was a picture of desolation and she sat in silence, oblivious to the mayhem around her.

I knelt next to her and spoke in Italian.

'Are you OK, Emma?'

She said nothing.

'You're not, are you?'

She shook her head, eyes welling up.

'Shall we go and sit outside for a bit, eh?'

She nodded.

I gave Giulia the deck of coloured cards. 'Can you play the colours game with them for five minutes? We'll be outside.' She was Emma's best friend, and, even at her age, she knew what was going on and smiled, happy to be Philip's right-hand girl.

We sat outside in the corridor, listening to the cacophony coming from every class.

I counted to ten. A long time, perhaps, if you're seven and upset.

'You know,' I said, 'I'm very proud of you.'

She looked up at me but said nothing.

'That's seventy-eight per cent. That's very good. I think you should be proud too.'

'But everyone else has done better.' Her voice wavered.

'Hey, it doesn't matter. Sometimes this happens. Next time, maybe you'll be top, next year.'

'But maybe I won't be here next year.'

'Why not?'

'Because maybe my dad will be cross.'

I knew her dad. A nice man who was not going to be cross.

'I bet you he won't be. I tell you what. When your dad comes to collect you, would you like me to speak with him? And I'll tell him how brilliant you've been and how proud I am of you. OK?'

'Really?'

'Really.'

She gave me the biggest smile I'd ever seen, and skipped into class without a backward glance, leaving me alone in the corridor. I counted to ten again, this time to stop myself from crying. I thought how I could not have done anything like this a year previously. I'd learned as much from them as they'd learned from me.

Final classes with kids were, in some ways, the toughest ones of the year. There was no work to be done, so it was a matter of keeping them entertained for ninety minutes. We played a lot of 'Fizz Buzz'. We played a lot of the colours game. We ate a lot of chocolate.

And then we were finished for the year. Very Little Emma was last to leave the class.

'Do you want me to speak to your dad?' I said.

She shook her head. 'It's OK.'

'Are you sure?'

She nodded and gave me a big smile. She showed me her certificate.

She'd done a good job, I have to give her that. She'd ever-so-carefully changed her mark so that 78 per cent had become 88 per cent.

I took a closer look at it. Her 'correction' looked indistinguishable. Nobody would notice. Unless they were told.

I really should not let this pass, I thought. I should have a word with Dad, and explain the whole thing, and it will be OK. I know it's not a proper exam, but I can't let her get away with this or she'll learn all sorts of bad lessons about how life works. Was I going to be so unprofessional?

She smiled up at me. She'd been a great kid, all year. And she looked so happy.

Oh hell.

'I'll see you next year, Emma,' I said.

'Will you be our teacher next year? Promise?'

'I promise.'

'And after?'

'I'll be your teacher as long as you want me to be, Emma.'

She was silent, and then threw her arms around my knees and hugged me. She skipped out of the room, her certificate in hand, to where her dad was waiting. I closed my eyes and counted to ten.

I never received presents when I worked in IT. I might have got a free meal and a boozy night out at the end of a project, but that's not the same. Teaching was different. By the end of that school year I'd received: a magnum of prosecco, a small green nodding turtle, a packet of Violetta paper handkerchiefs (it's the thought that counts), a photocopy of a book on Buddhist philosophy, a bag of chocolate Easter eggs, and a handmade card that read 'I love Inglish' (a present that delighted and yet disappointed in equal measure). I liked the turtle best. Nobody at the bank had ever bought me a turtle.

My adult elementary class took me for a meal after the last lesson. They'd been a lovely class, and one of the high points of the year. Everybody got on well, people had a laugh, and even the weaker ones had come on. There was one lesson left in the book to do. One final two-hour lesson and we could all break up for the summer. Surely, this time, I could get away without doing any prep?

I opened the book, and realised I'd made a terrible mistake. The last lesson was an introduction to the bloody Present Perfect. The Present Perfect is a sod to teach. It has no equivalent in Italian so you can't directly translate from one language to the other. What the hell was this doing here, tucked away at the end of the book? And why hadn't I spent more time on prep so I could have swapped in something else? I briefly wondered if I could teach them the words and actions to 'Up, Up and Away'. All I could do was plough through it and hope it didn't scar them too much . . .

Giovanni looked beaten by the end of the evening. He worked as a hairdresser in Mestre and didn't really need English for work as he had few non-Italian clients. He was studying because he thought it might be useful on holidays. He'd started with next to no knowledge of the language, but, by now, we could have a reasonable conversation together and he was always in good humour. Tonight, however, he looked as if he'd been in a fight. '*Ci hai ucciso stasera*,' he said. You have killed us this evening. I was worried that the offer of dinner was going to be withdrawn, but then he smiled. 'From now on, everything in Italian. *Vendetta*!'

We needed two cars to get to the restaurant, and Sergio gave me a lift in his. He'd worked hard all year, to the extent that he wanted an extra conversation class with me, during which we'd happily discuss the golden age of Italian football and great progressive rock bands of the past.

We drove into the country. We travelled quite a distance and I was starting to wonder if I'd pushed them too far and at any moment the car was going to pull over and they'd start digging a shallow grave. I saw an elderly lady crossing the road ahead of us. Sergio hadn't noticed.

Time stopped.

I wanted to scream but I couldn't think of the word "Stop!" in Italian. I realised I couldn't even think of it in English. We were about to take the life of an old woman because I couldn't think of the word 'Stop' in any language at all. All I could come up with was a strangulated 'NGARRGHHH!' as I flapped helplessly at the dashboard. And somehow it worked. Brakes slammed on and we screeched to a halt. The old lady didn't even break her stride . . .

I was expecting a beer and a pizza. I'd have been happy with a beer and a pizza. But what we sat down to was a four-course meal of exceptional quality, with not a few glasses of wine, and coffee and grappa. Everyone said they'd be back in the autumn. Sergio told an outrageous story involving Pink

Floyd and a motorcycle, which was too good not to be true and, surely, deserved to be written up as a short story . . .

Someone asked, 'Will you still be our teacher next year, Philip?' Just as Very Little Emma had done.

Of course I would. I wasn't going to let anyone else steal them.

Later that evening, as I walked – reasonably steadily – over the Calatrava bridge, I reflected on the past school year. I'd earned next to nothing. But I had students who bought me nice meals, packets of handkerchiefs and small nodding turtles. I was, by any reasonable definition, a lucky man.

Summer stretched out before us again, but it was going to be a busy one. The new flat needed work, starting with the kitchen. I could see us taking another trip to IKEA in Padua, but tried not to think about it.

The ancient, hand-painted, mustard-coloured fridge had given up the ghost and the landlord had agreed to buy us a new one. We'd already been around some of the electrical shops in Venice, but Caroline thought it might be worth going to the bigger stores in Mestre to have a proper look round.

We made our way to Piazzale Roma to take the free bus that would take us to Panorama and SME. It was early in the morning, but already felt oppressively hot and humid.

My mobile rang. A UK number that I recognised. My cousin.

'Cathy?'

'Phil. Are you all right . . .?'

At 9.30 in the morning, while waiting to go to Mestre to buy a fridge, I heard that my sister had died.

*   *   *

'The cars have arrived,' said Caroline. 'We won't be leaving for another ten minutes, but maybe we should go outside and take a look. Maybe it'll be less of a shock.'

Mum and Dad had already left for the church. I was glad of that. There would be friends waiting for them, they'd be looked after.

I went outside. Feeling OK; shaky, but in control.

There were floral tributes from the family in the hearse. A wreath in the shape of the Welsh flag. I spotted ours, with our card attached. I'd initially thought of a few lines from John Donne, but Caroline's suggestion of Dylan Thomas's 'And death shall have no dominion' was a better one. And then, the coffin. Covered in a Welsh flag.

Helen Susan Noble. 1968–2014. My sister.

I went inside. Still OK. Just about. Not much time for more than a few deep breaths, and to splash my face with cold water. It was time to go.

The church was lovely. Her husband, somehow, read the eulogy. More than that, he did it brilliantly. And then it was my turn. Ecclesiastes 3:1–6. *To everything there is a season.* The verses, so familiar, can easily sound like a banal shopping list of the obvious. I tried to dig deep into the words, wresting the meaning from them. Because they aren't banal at all, but perhaps the most beautifully concise expression of our journey through life ever written.

Readings, poetry, personal memories, everywhere faces etched with pain. The final hymn was, of course, 'Guide me, oh thou Great Redeemer'.

We moved to the cemetery for the interment. It was a beautiful spot. In an adjacent field a man was racing a pony and trap. The coffin, still covered in its flag, was lowered down. So small. Surely, I thought, surely, she was taller than this? I picked up a handful of earth, kissed the back of my hand, and cast it in. I think I said something, but can no longer remember the words. I brushed the dirt from my hands and walked away.

The wake was easier. All those friends and relatives and lots of happy memories. There were people I hadn't seen since our wedding. All those years, and this is what it took to bring us together again.

I knew her for forty-five years. There was never a moment in my life in which I was not aware of her being. Yet I have to admit that I did not know her as well as her friends and new family. For the last twenty-five years we had lived hundreds, sometime thousands of miles apart. She knew almost everything of interest about me yet there were sides of her that I knew nothing about. I should have made those calls, written those letters, sent those texts . . .

I expected the next morning to be easier, but slept badly. Music and words from the funeral echoed through my head all night long. I drove Caroline to Luton airport, feeling raw, bruised, fragile. I was going back to Wales to meet some old friends for the weekend, but it didn't seem right. We should, surely, be going home together. She gave me a hug. 'You need to do this. This will do you good.' Hugs and kisses and I drove off.

I was tired so I took it carefully. Hours of driving along anonymous motorways. I channel-surfed between Radios 3 and 4, but nothing engaged me. Helen became ill a year before we came to Venice, but she had always been so supportive of us. 'You have to go,' she told us. 'You might only have the one chance. Look what happened to me . . .'

And then something wonderful occurred. At the precise moment of crossing into Wales, Vaughan Williams's spectral *Fantasia on a Theme by Thomas Tallis* came on the radio. The sky cleared, and the hilly landscape of Powys unfolded before me. So lovely, I thought. Equal to anything back home. I wiped away another tear. In thirty minutes there would be the company of friends and laughter. And at that moment, at that perfect moment, it felt good to be alive.

Chapter 21

Life went on, of course. There was still a fair amount of work to be done on the flat, and it was good to have a few projects on the go to occupy my mind. We needed to get the kitchen sorted, make the spare room usable and put my *Doctor Who* DVDs into chronological order.

We've always been cat people, but it had been years since we'd last had one. Koritsi, an elderly black moggy passed on to us by his grateful previous owner, had turned out to be a misanthropic ball of grumpiness and spite who disliked the company of dogs, other cats, human beings and the animal kingdom in general. Naturally, I loved him to bits. He'd long since passed on, but – scarred by the experience – we'd never got another. We were settled now, though, and thought the time had come to try again.

The Dingo Venezia charity attempts to rehouse unwanted pets and strays, and *La Nuova* newspaper used to run a 'cute cat in desperate need of a home' feature every week. We also browsed Subito.it, an online equivalent of the *Exchange & Mart*, which led us to a cattery in Campodarsego, a small town on the outskirts of Padua. A town almost impossible to reach by public transport. As we trudged the last mile and a half, on one of the hottest days of the year, I started to think that these cats had better be suitably grateful.

We wanted a black cat, of course. Not for any nefarious or sorcerous reason, but because we wear a lot of black. The only one on offer – a kitten of three months, described as *furbo* ('crafty') – didn't want to know us. I picked him up, he scrabbled away furiously, and I let him drop before any major arteries could be severed. He'd blown his chance. His brother, however, was possibly the nicest cat in the world. He just wanted to be cuddled and have a good old purr. But he was still a kitten. He wanted to be running around doing mad stuff and breaking things. He wouldn't be ideal for a flat.

Elsewhere, Caroline had found a modestly friendly older kitten. He showed no objection to being picked up. He seemed to love it. He loved it so much that he never wanted to let go and his claws were locked on. Caroline was oblivious, but I noticed that he'd actually drawn blood. Her upper arm was bleeding on to the cat. Not just on a dark part either, but on the white bits. We detached him, and set him down; hoping that nobody would notice. *Blood on the cats*, as Bob Dylan almost wrote.

The final one was an adult of eighteen months. Her previous owner had died so, from being an only cat with an elderly lady owner, she found herself in a relatively confined space, surrounded by a host of rampaging and noisy kittens. She seemed gentle and good-natured, and yet terribly sad . . .

It had to be one of them . . . but which one?

That evening I found myself walking to the *Festa di Liberazione*, the annual celebration of the Refounded

Communist Party, resplendent in my best Che Guevara T-shirt and carrying a shocking pink cat basket. I think I cut a *bella figura*.

Of course we chose the sad cat.

We brought her home from Campodarsego. She whinged a bit on the way but mostly she was as good as gold. She hid behind the washing machine when we got her home, but not for long.

We needed a name. At the cattery they told us that the previous owner had got her gender wrong and called her Pippo. A perfectly good name, except that it's a boy's name and the diminutive of mine. To name a cat after yourself would seem an act of extreme egotism, and we'd have to explain the gender mix-up every time we introduced her. We tried to come up with something that sounded similar so she'd get used to it. I thought of Mimi. The sad heroine of *La Bohème* seemed appropriate for a slightly sad cat.

We were back at the Communist festival a few days later. This time without the pink cat basket. The festival hasn't been on for a couple of years now, which is a great shame as it was my favourite one in Venice, and Campo San Giacomo dell'Orio is probably my favourite square. You got a serious discussion followed by a band and, chances are, you'd buy a bottle of wine for five euros. There was even merchandise – The Struggle needs to move with the times, after all – so I bought an Antonio Gramsci fridge magnet, and Caroline a Bella Ciao T-shirt. I can't remember what the serious discussion was about. But I remember the band . . .

In 1971, Jethro Tull released the album *Aqualung*, one of the highlights of what would become a near forty-year career. At the time, the headline 'Jethro – now the world's biggest band?' appeared in the *New Musical Express* (and everybody believes what they read in the *NME*). The album has since sold over seven million copies. Not bad for a concept album where the central figure is a slightly-more-than-sleazy tramp, which compares the positive aspects of religious belief against the bad things that happen when such belief becomes institutionalised, and which is performed by a band who would not be allowed on television today for fear of frightening the children.

Drummer Clive Bunker left the band shortly afterwards. He was getting married and, rather sweetly, wanted to spend more time at home instead of being constantly on the road. It's a fair bet he never envisaged that, one day, he'd be the special guest star in a Tull tribute band in front of an audience of a couple of hundred Venetian Communists.

Friday night was a leaving party for one of our teaching colleagues, Chris, who was returning to the UK after two years in Venice. He had a PGCE, and had decided it was time to go home and look for a regular job in a primary school. He was young when the Tull were old, but didn't object to going along. The band – for an old Tull fan such as myself – were somewhere between fantastic and magnificent. What we got were the best bits from the albums *Stand Up* and *Aqualung* along with a suite from *Thick as a Brick* and, wonderfully, my favourite ever track, 'Hunting Girl' from *Songs from the Wood* (at which point, I must confess, Extreme Dad Dancing might have occurred).

The musicians were first class, the singer made a good attempt at Ian Anderson's voice, and Clive – well, Clive is a better drummer now than he was when he was famous. I hadn't seen him since the Tull's twentieth anniversary reunion in 1988. Today he resembles a dapper Spike Milligan. At the end of the gig, he engaged in a ten-minute Battle of the Drummers with the band's regular *batterista* (a very good young lad who, at the end, bowed before the wise old master). I enjoyed the evening far more than the last time I saw the actual band. All those old songs seemed fresh and new. There was the feeling that everybody was having the time of their lives.

I tried not to be too much of a fanboy, but I waited for Clive to come off stage and shook his hand. 'That was fantastic, mate,' I babbled. If he was surprised at my accent, he didn't show it. 'Well thank you very much, sir!' he said. With that, this modest man of rock made his way into the night.

Chapter 22

I should have learned my lesson.

When we first arrived in Venice, 'no job too small' had been an admirable motto. A few years down the line, and it had become a millstone. I found it impossible to turn work down.

I was already working a full working week when the position of *lettore* became available at a *scuola superiore* in Venice. This was everything I'd been looking for. It was a good job, regular hours and well paid, and it was in Venice. If I could get myself established there, I might not have to work on the mainland in future.

There was one problem. I already had a year's contract with the language school in Mestre. As well as the evening classes, I was getting sent out to Spinea for *lettore* work and after-school classes.

I looked at the expected hours in Venice. I looked at my existing timetable. It was just about physically possible. I submitted my CV, assuming I wouldn't get it.

I did. And then I had to make it work.

I demonstrated to the teaching world that it was possible to finish classes in Venice at eleven o'clock and make it to Spinea in time for a class at midday. It worked like this: making sure I had my coat, hat and bag ready for the bell at eleven, I would run to the Rialto vaporetto stop to get a boat up the Grand Canal. Delays could be frequent around Piazzale Roma due to the weight of traffic and so I would get off one stop early, at Ferrovia, and run along the *fondamenta* and over the Calatrava bridge. With a minute or two to spare, I would get on the direct bus to Spinea where, upon arrival, I would run from the bus stop to school. If everything went to plan I arrived precisely on time. If anything went wrong – an accident on the roads, a delayed vaporetto, or just a group of tourists dawdling and blocking the street – I wouldn't make it.

I did this for almost five months. I do not want to do it again.

The weeks were a hallucinatory blur of fifteen-hour days interspersed with half-hearted attempts at cooking and not enough sleep. I vaguely remembered that I had a wife. I wondered if I would ever see her again?

Why am I doing this? Seriously, why am I doing this?

Because you're in Venice.

The only reason I know I'm in Venice is the Marangona bell, chiming at midnight to remind me that I'm not going to get enough sleep.

Fridays were better. An early start but an earlier finish too, albeit with a difficult class (loveliness:unloveliness rating 60:40, a ratio that only needed a couple of absentees to ensure the week spiralled into chaotic miserableness). A few of us would have a beer in the bar over the road, before I headed to the regular Friday-night rehearsal with the Ensemble Vocale di Venezia.

That evening was different. I got off the tram and noticed my friends ahead. I strode to catch them up, and one of them turned to me:

'Ah! Nosferatu!'

I was a bit taken aback (although, in my heart of hearts, just a little bit pleased).

Was it because I seemed to have appeared out of nowhere? Was it the long coat (which, with your eyes half-closed, resembled the one worn by Max Schreck in Murnau's film)? Or were the endless 6 a.m. starts beginning to take their toll?

There were drinks and snacks at the end of the rehearsal, and Caroline had left a pasta sauce out for when I got home. I went to bed and read H. P. Lovecraft's *The Shadow over Innsmouth*. It's still scary after all these years, even in Italian. I heard the bells chiming midnight and decided I should get some sleep. I was working a six-day week, and Saturday classes, like all the others, were early starts. Then something plopped on to the end of the bed. There was a kick against the mattress, and a scrabbling of claws against wood . . .

Mimi the cat had taken to sleeping on top of the wardrobe. There was nothing wrong with this although once she was up there we never knew when she'd come down, hurling herself with deadly force onto our sleeping bodies in the small hours of the morning.

Like Lovecraft's narrator, I lay awake, listening for the telltale creak, the unexpected movement that reveals Something Bad is About to Happen.

And then the alarm was bleeping for 6 a.m. I showered and shaved, and gazed at the stranger in the mirror. Three months had turned me into Klaus Kinski.

I made a coffee and called it breakfast. It was still dark outside, as I made my way to Piazzale Roma, onto the bus and over the bridge to the Land of Shadows . . .

I held down two jobs for much of that school year. November to May does not sound like a long time. But when you've made it to the end of the first month and realise there are still over five months to go it seems like it's never going to end.

I staggered to the end of that year. I never ate breakfast, and rarely made time for lunch. Coffee substituted for food. Weight was dropping off me, which I was quite pleased about, yet a brief look in the mirror reminded me that I wasn't looking good. I only ever saw Venice from the inside of a classroom.

There was something about going into class, however, that made the adrenaline kick in. As soon as the lesson ended I would crash, but a free coffee from the machine – or sometimes two, or three – would be enough to get me through the next hour. I could not remember not being tired.

One evening, while cooking dinner, I went to change the bin liner in the pedal bin. It had been overfilled and, as I attempted to tie it up, the bottom ripped through depositing teabags, vegetable peelings and rotting fishbones over the floor.

Time seemed to stand still. All I could hear in my head were the words of 'Private Hell' by the Jam. And then I dropped to my knees and sobbed.

Mimi came running. She sat next to me while I crouched with my head in my hands, and miaowed piteously, jabbing at me with a paw, wanting to know what was going on.

Caroline arrived, and hugged me, sat me down, and let me cry. She told me I was never going to do this again. No more Mestre. No more Spinea. Just Venice. One school. No more commuting.

It made sense. By now I had enough experience on my CV to be able to work fewer hours for the same money. But I knew I'd miss my brilliant adult students. I'd miss Margherita, Giulia, Valentina, Alessandra, Francesca and Very Little Emma. I'd miss going to Spinea – I knew all the teachers there by now, and felt like I belonged. I'd taught every single kid in the school, and the first-year classes had all been lovely. I'd been looking forward to teaching them for the next two years.

Caroline told me firmly that no matter how lovely they might be, I was not going to do this again. And she was right. It was a foul job clearing up the rubbish, but there was some sense of a weight being lifted.

It wasn't just me. Caroline had collapsed in floods of tears over the office photocopier a week previously. I, at least, had the consolation of enjoying my job. She didn't even have that. It was time to start spreadsheet-pounding again. We were paying less rent now. Caroline could go part-time. It would just about work and we would never have to go through this again.

There were a couple of months remaining in the school year. It broke my heart to tell my teaching colleagues, my little girls and my schoolkids that I wouldn't be seeing them next year.

School came to an end in early June. It was tempting, oh so tempting, to sign up for another year. There were times when

I wavered, but Caroline was on hand to keep me strong, and I'd finally given in my notice. The third-year classes in Spinea were about to move up to *scuola superiore*. Living where they did, it was unlikely any of them would end up studying in Venice, and so it was unlikely I would teach any of them again. That made me a little bit sad.

We were in the middle of a lesson, with the kids working away on an exercise. The *professoressa* turned to me.

'You know the boys in 3A . . .?'

Of course. The rocker boys. They were only fourteen years old, but were into music that was old when I was young. Led Zeppelin, Black Sabbath, Pink Floyd. Every lesson we ended up talking about music, and about their band.

'It's the school concert in a couple of weeks. They asked me to ask you if you'd like to sing with them. The Rolling Stones, "Satisfaction".'

Well now.

I'd got my Saturday mornings back after six months of hard work. Did they seriously think I was going to give one up to make a two-hour round trip, for three minutes of singing, in a school concert for parents?

Yes. Yes, I was. Of course I was.

Caroline gave me some essential advice. Do not scowl.

'Do I scowl?'

'Yes, you do. You always look fierce when you sing. You'll frighten the children. And their parents.'

'It's serious music.'

'This is the Rolling Stones in a school concert. It's not Wagner.'

'Fair point. Anything else?'

266

'On no account try and imitate Mick Jagger.'

I headed off on Saturday morning with the words of 'Satisfaction' endlessly looping in my head, along with the words *Do not scowl. Smile. Do not attempt to imitate Mick Jagger.*

Everybody crammed into the gym, maybe fifty kids and a hundred parents. Most of the concert was made up of familiar classics and pop songs, played by an army of descant recorders. Carmen read some poetry. Eleonora played violin. And then, at the end, Gianmarco (bass), Francesco (guitar), Lorenzo (drums) and *Professore Mr Jones* stood up . . .

I did not scowl. I smiled. I did not attempt to imitate Mick Jagger. And I successfully fought any temptation to dance.

And it was pretty good. I looked at the parents. They were laughing – in a good way – smiling and clapping. The lads in the band gave me a big grin. I looked out at the rest of the kids, armed with their recorders. Three years together, and this was the last time. I was so, so proud of them. Of all of them.

I've been fortunate enough to sing in some of the greatest spaces in Venice. But a school gym in a small provincial town was perhaps the most special of all.

Chapter 23

I read the email again. A literary agent had bought my self-published (and half-forgotten) *The Venice Project* and enjoyed it. He wanted to know what I was working on.

This was flattering but more than a little scary. Mainly because I wasn't working on anything at all. I had fragments of ideas for a crime novel set in contemporary Venice, but nothing I could justify with the word 'plot'. I didn't know if I'd get around to writing it but, if I did, I'd assumed I'd self-publish again.

It was at least an idea that I could talk about. But I thought I needed to be very cool about this. It would be best not to sound too enthusiastic. I should wait a little before replying.

I gave it about five minutes.

We spoke on the telephone a few days later. I was at an outdoor swimming pool, near Mirano, where Caroline and I would escape from the crowds and the heat of the city. I got on well with the agent (I'm pleased to say I still do), ran through the few ideas I had, and he asked me to send him three chapters by the end of the month.

I had no plot, no characters and I had never written, or attempted to write, a novel before. It was almost certainly going to come to nothing. But this was a contact with an actual literary agent, one who sounded enthusiastic about the few details I'd give him.

It was exciting. I finished my lunchtime beer and jumped in the swimming pool realising, too late, that I had just taken my mobile phone for our first-and-last swim together.

One month, then, to write the best three chapters of my life. Or, given that I'd never written a novel before, the first three chapters of my life. What did I have?

I sketched out a contemporary crime thriller set in Venice. I thought back to our visit to the bank in Campo Manin. A prayer book that might be by Giovanni Bellini, currently held under lock and key. That was a start.

The protagonist, a policeman? Too difficult. I had no idea how on earth one might go about researching how the police system worked. There was information on the internet, but I wasn't sure that would be sufficient. Besides, I didn't think I could write convincingly from the point of view of an Italian, let alone a Venetian. He'd have to be British.

Then I remembered the Honorary Consul. Every week I would arrive for our English lesson and find him trying to extricate visiting tourists from whatever tricky situation they'd managed to get themselves into. This was a job where you'd have contacts in the police, in the church and in the various strata of Venetian society. That was the solution!

He'd need a sidekick. I didn't like the idea of him being happily married or settled down. He'd live alone. On the Street of the Assassins, naturally. He'd need somebody to speak to when he got home.

Mimi perched on the sofa behind me, and miaowed. I scratched her behind her ears, and she closed her eyes and purred. What a good little cat she was. Unlike our last one . . . *unlike our last one . . .*

It wasn't much, but it was a start. The British Honorary Consul in Venice, alone save for his unfriendly cat, is drawn into the theft of a prayer book by Giovanni Bellini; and somewhere I needed to incorporate a story about Pink Floyd and a vintage motorcycle.

I put together three chapters, and sent them off.

The reply was positive, and effectively ended with the words 'Great, now send me the rest of it.' All I had to do now was to stick another 80,000 words on the back of what I'd already written, and 80,000 words seem like quite a lot when you've never done it before.

I stuck with it over the next three months. I made myself write one thousand words a day, and it started to take shape. Caroline read it through and liked it, even if we will never agree on the use of the Oxford comma. I sent it off and waited. I was prepared for a polite rejection.

Two weeks passed and then the email arrived. The literary agent liked it. More than that, he loved it and wanted to represent me. I bounced around the room, hugging Caroline and Mimi. Caroline was almost as excited as me. Mimi took it in her stride.

There was, my agent – how I loved saying that – reminded me, a long way to go. He also gave me some very good advice: do not get excited. I managed not to. I had not come to Venice to write a book. I enjoyed my job, I was blessed with a lovely wife and had a cat who quite liked me. If it didn't work out, I told myself, I was still a lucky man. I had enough.

There were, of course, a few rejections; always polite and along the line of 'we like this but it's not for us'. I tried not to let them get me down. This was my first novel, I had an agent and that was further than most writers get. I was aware that it might not happen.

And then it did.

On 25 September 2015, an email arrived with the words 'Get the prosecco out!' We'd done it. I had a two-book contract with Little, Brown under the Constable imprint (I was particularly thrilled to discover I now had the same publisher as Bram Stoker). We'd have to wait until 2017 for publication but I didn't care. I emailed and telephoned everybody I could think of. I hugged Caroline (I do this quite often, not just when I have a contract for a book) and told Mimi she was going to be a Famous Cat. She took that in her stride, as well. Wonderfully, our Brilliant Australian Friends were visiting and we went out to celebrate with Negronis at the bar on the Street of the Assassins.

Nathan Sutherland, Honorary Consul in Venice, made his debut in *The Venetian Game* in 2017, and returned for *Vengeance in Venice* a year later. Italian translations and audiobooks followed, and suddenly I was signing copies in bookshops and replying to emails from complete strangers.

The next few years will see *The Venetian Masquerade* and a fourth – as yet untitled – Nathan novel. It seems crazy but then everything does these days, whether it be writing a series of crime novels, singing in the Scuola Grande di San Rocco or teaching small children.

I am, I suppose, an accidental novelist. I am also a very fortunate one, in that my little self-published book fell into the hands of the right person. I wish I could give some advice for aspiring writers but, really, I'm not the best person for that. All I can say is this: telling stories is a pretty cool thing to do. Keep writing. Because everyone should have a day in their life when they receive an email that begins with the words 'Get the prosecco out!'

Epilogue

S even years have passed since we got out of a water
taxi with ten pieces of luggage and sat outside a bar
in an increasingly chilly Campo San Barnaba, trying not
to become too concerned as the shadows lengthened and
the agent for our flat obstinately refused to answer the
phone.

Jan Morris memorably described the experience of living
in Venice as one of the greatest pleasures that life can offer.
Caroline's description of our first few years is more prosaic,
but heartfelt: 'I didn't expect it to be difficult.' There is truth
in both these viewpoints.

It's not like being on permanent holiday. After the initial
excitement of those first few heady months, no matter how
well you think you know a place as a visitor, it will be very
different as a resident. There will be a culture shock.

When we'd settled in, there were weeks – even months –
when we did nothing more interesting than working or
preparing for work. As we toiled away at lesson plans late at
night, while the rain hammered on the dark streets outside, it
was easy to think we could be anywhere. 'New Life' was, in
many ways, similar to 'Old Life'.

But there were also those moments on a late-night vaporetto, where the only thing to be seen on the Grand Canal was the silhouette of a lone gondolier, and we would think ... *Bloody hell ... this is where we live!* Or travelling to work on a crowded boat on a cold and dark January morning, and seeing the sun start to rise over the Rialto Bridge. Whether it be buying fish from the Rialto market, listening to a concert at the church of the Frari, watching the shadows lengthen on the Giudecca canal or drinking Negronis that taste like a friendly slap in the face as the evening crowds go by on their *passeggiata*; there is something about this city that knocks the cynicism out of you. There is still a magic to it and that magic can change you.

Should you try something like this yourself? I hope this book goes some way towards answering that question. We got away with it, but not everybody will. Don't attempt it in the hope of patching up a marriage or relationship: you'll end up divorced within the first year. Be prepared for the culture shock. Plan for inevitably spending more money than you thought. And there will be bad times, dark nights of the soul when the thought *Have we made a terrible mistake?* creeps into your head and refuses to go away.

Take the trouble to learn Italian. Your enjoyment of the experience will be in direct proportion to your knowledge of the language. You can get by with a rudimentary grasp in a city such as Venice, but you will never feel at home. A common language will open up culture and literature, newspapers and news and enable you to make Italian friends. And friends will make the difference.

Lovely as it is, there is a sadness to Venice. The city is not sinking – at least not to a degree that will affect anyone reading this book in their lifetime. The problem is emigration. In Campo San Bartolomeo, a chemist's shop displays an LED screen which shows the population of the city. At the time of writing, it stands at fewer than fifty-five thousand. Fifty years ago, it would have been double that. As property prices increase, rents become unaffordable for locals. If you happen to have inherited a property from your parents, the temptation is to sell up and move to the mainland where you can buy a bigger house for less money. Living on the mainland allows you to have a car and, with your own means of transport, the range of work available increases. Add to this the day-to-day difficulties of living in a small city jammed with thousands of tourists – the packed streets, the overcrowded vaporetti, the closing of useful shops to be replaced with souvenir outlets – and you start to understand why, year on year, the population grows ever smaller.

I have, by my reckoning, taught about 1 per cent of the city's population. Include their parents, people I sing with, friends of friends and expats, and you might think I would constantly be running into people I know around the town. This doesn't happen very often. Locals are hugely outnumbered by visitors. Residents can pass through the crowds almost unnoticed, veritable 'Anonymous Venetians'.

Yet despite its decline and its image as a 'museum city', Venice has never been afraid of embracing the new. The city has reinvented itself – if not to everybody's taste – as a capital of contemporary culture: scarcely a month goes by without some kind of celebration of music, architecture, film, dance or art.

Perhaps, then, everyone is being too pessimistic. There are still schools, universities and plenty of young people. The glory days of the city were well over four hundred years ago and people were probably moaning then that it wasn't what it used to be.

Will we ever feel like Venetians? I don't think so. We came here too late in life for that. However good our Italian (or *Veneziano*) may get, our accents will mark us out. I can imagine going into a restaurant in twenty years time, being addressed in English and given a tourist menu. It is part of the nature of living here.

I feel as if we've run across a busy road and got away with it, because there was never any guarantee that The Venice Project was going to succeed. I thought there was a reasonable chance that it *might*, but I was prepared for not finding sustainable work and treating the experience as a year off before trying somewhere else in Italy. Or, in the worst case, come crawling back to the UK and do whatever it is that de-skilled middle-aged IT workers do in the middle of an economic crisis.

I'm fortunate to be able to spend most of my time writing, but I still teach and hope I will always want to. It's been good to me. Caroline restricts herself to translation work and occasional art history classes in English, and is much the happier for it. Mimi sleeps and eats, and lives what is a very enviable lifestyle.

Part of me regrets that we will never again experience waiting for our flight from Heathrow and realising that for the first time in our adult lives we no longer possessed a key for anything; or of waking up to the sound of the bells of the

Carmini the following morning, with the future seeming full of possibilities. Yet how fortunate we are to have had such experiences at all.

Venice gave us a second chance. It gave us back our self-belief, and pushed us to do things we would never have thought possible. Most importantly, it taught us that we could do more, with less. We came to Venice in search of a better, simpler life. We were wrong about the 'simpler' bit, and we are the better for it.

So here we still are, in the middle of an adventure when we'd never expected to have one again. I know that I'm a different person to the one that left Edinburgh. I hope I'm a better one. This book, then, has been a love letter to a city to which we owe everything.

We have been lucky in many ways. I hope that you'll be lucky too.

I hope that one day you also meet a Man in a Pub.

Glossary

Detailed here are those terms not directly explained in the text itself. For reasons of clarity, I have used the Italian spelling instead of the Venetian whenever a choice exists.

ACTV: Azienda del Consorzio Trasporti Veneziano, the company responsible for public transportation throughout Venice and Mestre.

Acqua alta: literally 'high water', usually in spring or autumn and due to a combination of high tides, the phase of the moon and prevailing winds from the south.

Alilaguna: the waterbus service that runs from Marco Polo airport into Venice itself.

Altana: a wooden terrace erected above a rooftop, serving as an outside seating area.

Bacino: the wide expanse of water in front of the ducal palace, where the Grand Canal and Giudecca canal widen into the lagoon; often referred to as the Bacino di San Marco.

Borsa crolla: 'stock market collapses', often seen paired with '*lo spread vola*' ('the spread widens'), a headline that became distressingly familiar both before and after our move to Italy.

Calle (pl. *calli*): Venetian name for a street or alley.

Campo: literally 'field', the name given to squares and public spaces throughout the city; Piazza San Marco is the notable exception.

Il Cavaliere: 'the cavalier', a common nickname for Silvio Berlusconi, used by friends and enemies alike.

Cellulare: a mobile phone, sometimes called a *telefonino* (literally 'little phone').

CELTA: Certificate in English Language Teaching to Adults.

Centrodestra: in political terms, the centre-right.

Centrosinistra: in political terms, the centre-left.

Centro storico: the historic centre, or oldest part, of a city.

Chiesa: church.

Cicchetti (**Venetian:** *cicheti*): small snacks, or finger food, served in traditional *bacari* (wine bars) or *cicchetterie*, from which one can construct a most satisfactory lunch.

Giardini: the public gardens in the east of the city; laid out during the Napoleonic period and used to host the Architecture and Art Biennales.

Lardo: a type of charcuterie made from the cured back fat of a pig.

Lettore/lettrice: literally, 'reader'; the title typically given to an English mother-language teacher in the state school system, somewhere between the responsibilities of a teacher and teaching assistant.

Liston: *far el liston*, in Venetian, is to take a *passeggiata* – a stroll or walk, typically through the main square.

Moka: the classic Italian stove-top coffee pot, designed by Alfonso Bialetti.

No Grandi Navi: literally 'no big ships'; an organisation campaigning against the passage of enormous, environmentally damaging cruise ships through the Giudecca canal and the *bacino*.

Padrone/padrona: landlord or landlady (I'm told the feminine form can also mean 'dominatrix' so it's as well to be careful while using this in conversation).

Passerelle: temporary raised walkways that allow the pedestrian to move around the city during periods of *acqua alta*.

Rinfresco: refreshments (in the sense of a celebration or reception).

Sacra Conversazione: literally 'Sacred Conversation'; typically, a depiction of the Madonna and Child in the company of a number of saints.

Seppie: cuttlefish.

La Serenissima: 'The most serene republic', an appropriate description of the Republic of Venice at the height of its power.

Sestiere: district or borough; the six *sestieri* of Venice are Cannaregio, Castello, San Marco, San Polo, Santa Croce and Dorsoduro.

La settima arte: 'the seventh art', i.e. film; a suitably reverential term given the Italian love of cinema.

Soppressa: a typical style of salami from the Veneto.

Sportello: a window or counter.

Straniero (**pl.** *stranieri*): a foreigner or stranger.

TEFL: Teaching English as a Foreign Language.

Terraferma: the mainland.

Tessera Sanitaria: Health Insurance Card.

Vaporetto: a boat that serves as a waterbus in the city.

Vongole: clams.

Further Reading

There is no shortage of reading material, both fact and fiction, about *La Serenissima*. The following is a selection of those books I have found particularly useful, and those that have given me the greatest pleasure.

Jan Morris, *Venice* (Faber & Faber, 1993): surely the most enthralling book ever written about the city; wonderfully literate and packed with information. Morris describes Venice at the end of the 1950s as a place of melancholy beauty. How I would have loved to have lived there at that time.

Marcel Proust, *In Search of Lost Time* (Vintage Classics, 1996): is there any better description of the experience of the first-time visitor to the city? Proust's Venice is possibly even more magical than the real thing.

Daphne du Maurier, 'Don't Look Now' (Penguin Modern Classics, 2006): claustrophobic, melancholy little chiller, originally published in the short-story collection *Not After Midnight*. I knew it better from Nicolas Roeg's film version (which, in Italian, has the marvellous title of *A Venezia . . . un Dicembre Rosso Shocking*) and was surprised to find

– upon rereading the original – that the iconic figure of the tiny assassin is only dressed in red in the movie. No matter. Read it. Watch it. Then walk the streets alone at night and try to keep the image of that little figure in red out of your mind . . .

Giorgio Vasari, *The Lives of the Artists* (Oxford World's Classics, 2008): Vasari never quite understood the art of *La Serenissima*, believing it fundamentally inferior to that of his native Florence. Nevertheless, his chapters on Venetian art, and his account of a visit to Titian in the company of Michelangelo, are well worth reading.

John Ruskin, *The Stones of Venice* (Penguin Classic History, 2001): sagacious, comprehensive in detail and often surprisingly witty and scathing, Ruskin's masterwork is perhaps more for dipping into than reading cover to cover, but it's a very useful reference work to have to hand.

H. C. Robbins Landon and John Julius Norwich, *Five Centuries of Music in Venice* (Thames & Hudson, 1991): a comprehensive history of Venetian music, recounted in great detail and with erudition.

Tiziano Scarpa, *Venice is a Fish* (Serpent's Tail, 2009): a quirky, humorous account of Venice and the Venetians from an excellent writer.

Caroline Prosser, *Living and Working in Italy* (Survival Books, 2011): the most useful book I found on the practicalities and problems of making a move to Italy.

The Silver Spoon (Phaidon, 2011): the alpha and omega of Italian cookery. The number of recipes packed into its 1500 pages can make it a dry read, but it's essential as a reference.

Francesco da Mosto, *Francesco's Kitchen* (Ebury, 2007): this is one of surprisingly few English language cookbooks dedicated to Venetian cuisine. Engagingly written, with plenty of history among the recipes.

Alan Davidson, *Mediterranean Seafood* (Prospect Books, 2012): a peerless guide to seafood cookery. Davidson details each species of fish, listing local names, together with a series of recipes. Comprehensive, informative and fascinating. Read it, even if you never cook a single recipe from it.

With Thanks

Caroline and I would like to thank the organisers and members of Spin, a contemporary art group run by the National Galleries of Scotland, without whom we might never have come to Venice in the first place.

To all those to whom we never got the chance to say goodbye – we're sorry. We simply ran out of time.

To those we've lost touch with over the years – again, we're sorry. We should have made more effort.

To those friends from our previous life at the bank – thank you for making things less horrible than they might otherwise have been. You know who you are.

We are enormously grateful to the Italian Cultural Institute of Edinburgh, who gave us a bursary to study at the Istituto Venezia; and to the Randolph School of Edinburgh, where we retrained in TEFL.

I would like to thank the teaching staff with whom I have had the pleasure of working over the past seven years, in particular Fabiola Capozzi, Nicoletta da Re, Elisabetta Battistel, Roberta Spina, Elisabetta Cognolato, Stefania Rizzo, Marina Curtolo, Martina Schultz and Michela Zernitz. Not forgetting the Oxford School of Mestre, and

Sandra, Daniela, Nick S, Nick J, Chris, Henry, Andrea and Clare.

To my lovely Thursday-night class – Margherita, Giulia, Valentina, Alessandra, Francesca and Very Little Emma – thank you from the bottom of my heart. I am, I hope, a better and kinder person for having been your teacher. I've changed your names but I hope you read this one day – in English, of course – and recognise yourselves.

To the Ensemble Vocale di Venezia – my love and thanks to my friends and co-singers Stefano Croce, Alvise Minghetti, Gianfranco Munerotto, Maurizio Gottardi, Francesco Tricco, Raphael Franco, Matteo Simone, Elisabetta Ferrari, Bettina Bettini, Marina Pastore, Silvia Laudati, Stefania Tiozzo, Antonella Roncaglione and not forgetting *maestro* Gianandrea Pauletta. Quite simply, you have made the difference. To the Cantori Veneziani – I'm sorry I don't have space to list everyone but I love you all!

To our brilliant Australian friends Peter and Louise Stockfeld – thank you for walking the walk with us. And for dragging our bookcases over the Calatrava bridge.

To the Man in the Pub – thank you, wherever you are.

My thanks, as ever, to my lovely, brave and brilliant wife Caroline without whom none of this would be happening. To my agent and friend John Beaton – thank you for picking up my little self-published book. Again, none of this would be happening without you. To my editor Martin Fletcher, Krystyna Green, Rebecca Sheppard, Andy Hine, Jess Gulliver and all at Little, Brown – my continued thanks for your wonderful work and support.

And finally, to those who expressed their support and offered all sorts of help when they heard what we were up to – a massive thank you. Without you, we might well have given up the whole idea as insane. It might very well have *been* insane, but we still did it. And no, we were not being brave – we just did something we really wanted to do.